THE FEMININE ENERGY GUIDE

FROM SELF-REJECTION TO CONSCIOUS CONNECTION

NIKI KINSELLA

Disclaimer

I have tried to recreate events, locales and conversations from my memories of them. In order to maintain their anonymity in some instances I have changed the names of individuals and places, I may have changed some identifying characteristics and details such as physical properties, occupations and places of residence.

ISBN13: 978-1-913728-47-2

CONTENTS

DEDICATION

I dedicate this book to you my Doris. My Mummypoos. My bestest friend I ever had. My guardian angel.

Losing you was the catalyst that changed my whole world.

You showed me what true strength and courage looked like. You taught me how to come from a place of unconditional love and kindness and how to always find the good in everything and everyone.

You are my inspiration.

I am so proud to call you my mum, and if I can be half the woman you were then I will have done an amazing job.

Love you forever and ever and ever!

Your shining star x

THE FEMININE ENERGY GUIDE

Hello you gorgeous human. I am so happy you have opened my book.

That place where you are right now, where you feel like you have had enough of people pleasing and putting up with other people's shit, of having to hold your tongue and walk on eggshells in case you upset someone. AND THEN, if you DO upset them having to pussy foot around them until they decide to stop being an absolute NOBEND to you...and all because you spoke your mind!

I know that where you are now it feels easier to stay small, to stay unseen, to not even bother trying to make changes and to stay safe in your comfort zone, but deep down inside I know that where you are now is NOT where you want to stay.

I know you want to feel free and fulfilled and confident to do all the things that make your soul feel alive, to wake up in the morning and feel like you are looking forwards to the day because you are living your BEST life doing the things that YOU want to do!

What if I told you that you have the power to change your reality? That YOU have the power to fulfil all your dreams and desires. That you CAN overcome your fears and negative beliefs that are holding you back?

That you can SET YOURSELF FREE FROM FEAR!

Close your eyes for a moment and just imagine for one moment that you can!

This book is for the woman who is scared but is also ready to make changes; ready to live life a different way. Ready to set herself free. Ready to implement well overdue boundaries and feel confident saying *No* to anything that does not light her up. Ready to build and boost her self-belief and self-worth by diffusing old limiting beliefs and stories that have triggered her and kept her in hiding for many years.

I want you to know that I have been where you are numerous times throughout my life, with different people that chose to see my good nature as a sign of weakness and take full advantage of me by almost destroying every last little sparkly bit of my soul.

I used to feel like a butterfly trapped inside a box, feeling completely suffocated and petrified. Fluttering around nervously in case I touched the edges and they heard me; always trying to look beautiful and please other people so they would love me.

So I want you to know that I GET IT!

I get that you are scared right now, but you can't go on anymore because it feels like it will kill you if you carry on ignoring how you feel. I get that you have had enough of doing the things that make other people happy. I get that you have had enough of keeping your dreams small just to please other people a but you are scared to be seen because of the fear of people laughing at you or judging you. I get that you are ready to make changes but don't know where to start and are absolutely shit scared of what is going to happen because you have always put other people's needs before your own.

I get this because not that long ago I was EXACTLY where you are now.

Unfortunately, it took the death of both of my parents and a worldwide pandemic for me to WAKE UP and realise that you only get one shot at this life; that actually this isn't a fucking dress rehearsal!

I am here to show you that you CAN make changes in your life, and that you are already enough exactly as you are.

And I get that because you have kids, and mountains of debt and three jobs and no time, and because of this and that and blah blah blah and all the other excuses you are trying to make because you are scared and don't know where to start, you feel you can't do the things you want to do.

I want you to know I have been there too and if I can do it, then YOU DEFINITELY CAN!

I have written this book to inspire all the women who have ever felt not good enough, too stupid, not confident enough, too fat, too ugly, indecisive, ashamed, guilty, undeserving, unlovable, rejected, in a state of feeling frozen with fear because you don't know what decision to make in case you upset your spouse, partner, mother, father, friend, colleague, neighbour, dog, cat or actual fucking universe itself!

I am here to take you on a journey of self-discovery to look deep inside of yourself so you can, maybe for the first time in your life, discover who you truly are, to feel how you truly feel and for you to know that whatever this looks like for you, that this is okay.

I want you to do this so that you no longer feel disconnected from your life and from yourself.

So that you no longer feel like life is happening all around you and you're just going along for the ride. Like when you're a child buckled up in the back of your parent's car, just going where you are told to go. Even though you *reeeeeeeally don't want to go to grandma's house because she licks her lips before she puckers up with her little prickly old lady moustache and smooches you on the cheek*. But you don't get to choose because you just have to go.

Guess what? Now you CAN choose!

I used to feel like I had to still ask people if it was okay to do things even as an adult like I was not in control of my own life.

I felt like this my whole life, like I needed other people's approval or permission before I could make a decision. Why? This was my life, why was I constantly trying to please other people who often weren't even interested or had no idea what I was doing anyway, to help me make a decision. Or even sometimes make it for me!

One of the most pivotal moments in my life was when one of my coaches said to me,"You do NOT need permission!"

I felt like all my imaginary shackles instantly shattered off my body and each little piece turned into a butterfly and flew away onto the sky.

Looking back now I know the reasons why I was like this, which I will share with you throughout this book. Setting myself free from this type of pressure and confusion and self- entrapment changed my life more than I can even put into words!

I am going to show you how to truly connect to your beautiful self, by showing you how to strip back the noise of the world and of your peers, and of all the things that you have always been told are the truth and never questioned. To show you that you cannot get this wrong and that it is never too late to start again, to trust your own inner voice and to help you have the confidence to let it be heard, so that you can feel what is happening to you and make your own choices and decisions, instead of looking to others for approval and acceptance first.

And believe me, there is no better feeling that being connected to yourself. The clarity and confidence that this gives you in immeasurable.

Throughout the book I will be sharing with you the things that I know will help you, exactly why they will help you, and sharing some of my own gritty experiences to show you how I implemented these lessons into my life.

The lessons I know will help you to step out of your shadows and ignite the fire in your beautiful belly to live your life as the very best version of yourself.

I will show you that even when you feel like you are all the things I listed above earlier, and even when you think the worst thing in the world is happening to you, and there is no way out... that 99% of the time these are just stories that we are telling ourselves and you can do anything you put your mind to, that it is never too late to make changes, and that YOU DO NOT

NEED PERMISSION to do the things in life that make YOU happy! (And I can help you find these happy things too if you don't know what they are yet.)

Changing our mindset is the most challenging thing we can ever do. It is not an easy job to look at the way we are thinking, feeling and reacting to things in our lives. Also known as shadow work, and it's called this for a very good reason, it's bloody dark inside our minds.

Sometimes, we know we have been a bit of a knob and it feels really uncomfortable and sometimes even a bit scary, guilty, shamey and vulnerable to have to look at it all again.

We lock all sorts of things away in there don't we. All the stuff we don't want other people to know we are thinking and all the things that we have done that we never want to remember. But, remember this, you can NEVER fail at something because there is always a lesson in everything we do.

We can ALWAYS learn from these lessons.

Even when we sometimes have to repeat them painfully, and annoyingly many, many times, until we FINALLY GET THE FUCKING MESSAGE!

There is ALWAYS something to learn, and everything always happens for a reason.

I want you to remember that you have been put here on this little spinney planet for a reason. (This next bit might gross a few people out, but I'm not sorry because it explains perfectly what I need it too.) That out of the 40 trillion, quadrillion billion sperm that you were the one that made it. And just in case you didn't know, our little eggs don't just let any wriggler in, it has to be one that she connects too. So even before we became a conscious being, we were a smooth charismatic little wriggler who charmed its way into becoming human.

You are supposed to be here!

There is only one you!

And you have, and always will be enough!

We just need to work on removing some of the shit that has stuck to you from hateful, horrible things other people have said, or things you have been made to believe over time by society or your peers, so that you begin to believe this yourself and if you just think for a minute about how long you have been alive, about how many years that little icky bits of sticky shit will have actually stuck to you?

And all of the things you will have been told about how we should be doing this by now, or look like that, and be married with kids, and have a good job, and a mortgage, and a pension and be a size 10 with no wrinkles and beautiful long lush hair and a car and go on holiday and have savings and be happy. OH, MY ACTUAL FUCKING GOD! STOP PLEASE!

Pretty much my whole life I have people pleased, I did this because I was so scared of people not liking me or judging me or talking about me behind my back or not approving of what I was doing...and guess what...no matter what I did, they did it anyway!

Somebody will always have something to say about what you are doing. Somebody will always not like you no matter WHAT you do.

There's a well-known saying by the beautiful Dita Von Teese, "You can be the ripest, juiciest peach in the world but there will always be someone who hates peaches."

I haven't always felt confident, and I haven't always believed in myself. It took me a long time to get where I am now, and it was no walk in the park let me tell you. But I am here to show you that anything is possible.

When we can take our pain and turn it into purpose, that's when things start getting REALLY exciting. But first we need to feel it to heal it.

People think that healing is such a beautiful thing. That the process is hugs and resting and getting better and chatting with friends over cups of teas and them understanding what is going on for you, but the real truth is healing hurts like an absolute MOFO.

A MOFO that has cystitis, and piles.

And an ingrowing toenail.

And ulcers on the sides of their tongue that their teeth rub on every time they eat or talk.

And a big fuck of volcanic abscess in the crease of their ass.

And all of this while going backwards down a hill in a wheelbarrow!

That's what it really feels like.

But it's SOOOOOO worth it.

In this book I will share with you my spiritual toolkit that I have created along my journey so far (and also help you to create your own) of all the things that have helped me to not get in the cupboard with a bottle of vodka when shit was going on. And that is honestly what I used to do, any excuse to have a drink and I was there. And now I am proud to say I don't need to do that anymore.

I am not a guru.

I am definitely not putting myself on a pedestal.

I am just like you.

I am here in hope that I can inspire you in some little way to just step forward, to release fear and discover who you truly are so that you can shine your beautiful light into the world and live your happiest life and to pee glitter everywhere.

I am here to help you be the best version of yourself that you can be, to live your best and happiest life. I will guide you with love and support creating a safe and sacred space for you to start your journey. I know you can do this because I have done it, or rather, am still doing it. Sometimes all we need is someone to believe in us, and I BELIEVE IN YOU!

Are you ready change your life?

Let's do this!

INTRODUCTION

SHARING IS CARING

Hello my beautiful souls.

Before you start reading, I just wanted to explain the journey this book will take you on. This book is part autobiography and part inspirational/self-help/light a fire in your belly/make you want to shine your beautiful light out into the world.

At the start I will be sharing with you my own personal story about the things that have happened in my life, all the shit and the grit. The reason that I have done this is to show you that I can probably resonate with most of the shit that you have gone through or are going through in your life. That I am a real person, and not someone pretending to know everything and have a magic wand.

It's the difficult times that help us to grow, in ways we could only dream possible. And I believe that we are meant to go through all these dark times, to be cracked open, even though it hurts like hell, because that's how the light gets in.

I know first-hand how fucking hard it is when you want to make changes, I have fell off the wagon many times and rolled back down the hill to the bottom. Sometimes to even further away than where I was when I started. But I always got up again, pulled the twigs out my hair, dusted myself off, and started again. But the next time I always held on tighter.

After I have depressed the shit out of you and made you want to come and rescue me and hug me within an inch of my life, I will share with you the things that I found (or that found me) that have helped me to heal and change my life.

But most importantly how they helped me to find my souls purpose while I am here on this spinny little planet. How they helped me to feel connected and aligned and to trust myself implicitly so that I no longer looked to others to help me make decisions in my life anymore. Nor did I need their permission.

I feel more complete than I have ever done in my whole life and for me, it is all down to these things that I am about to share with you.

At the end of each section, I will give you little exercises for you to try out, so that you can really begin to practice implementing these things and bringing them into your life in a way that feels right for you.

Shall we begin?

1

TINY LITTLE PEOPLE PLEASER

I haven't always felt confident, and I haven't always believed in myself.

It took me a long time to get where I am now, and it was no friggin walk in the park let me tell you. People think that healing is such a beautiful thing, that the process is all hugs and resting and people caring for you and then you get better.

But the truth is healing is re-living all the shitty pain and waking up to the cold hard reality that some people on this planet are just narcissistic bastards – who don't have a soul or a single emotion in their body.

And they like it when you cry *because* of them.

My life started out being born to a shamed, single mother. My nan, my mum's mother, made it very clear that she did not approve of my biological dad, so was delighted when the pressure and constant reminder of what a disappointment they were bringing a bastard into the world made them go their separate ways.

On the night I was born my mum gave birth to me all alone in hospital. My nan couldn't be with her because she had had a drink and was a bit drunk. Looking back on this situation now, knowing what I know, before I was even born I was subject to the belief of not being good enough or worthy enough. A belief that I have struggled with my whole entire life and when my energy is low will pop its ugly little head up to try and remind me. This belief has been passed down to me from my mother and was pretty much programmed into my DNA before I had even taken my first breath. I will explain more about this later in the book.

My nan also made it clear that she did not care for crying babies in the house while she was trying to nap or watch her television shows.

And I cried A LOT!

My mum would have to take me out the house for a walk or drive round with me often for hours, because every time she stopped moving I would wake up and cry.

When I was three months old my mum weighed six and a half stone. She loved me with every cell in her being, but she was sad and alone and exhausted. Babies are very good at picking up on people's energy, and when the mamma is anxious and on edge, so is the baby. And so it cries.

I was born an empath. I felt everything from being teeny tiny, and the energy in that house could be described as nothing other than having to walk in eggshells. I apparently cried for the whole first year of my life my mum said, and I am 100% sure that it was because I was picking up on my poor mummypoo's vibes.

We lived there until I was four years old when my mum met and married my stepdad who then adopted me. My mum had my brother quickly after they married and I can remember feeling a bit pushed out. I was just a jealous little four-year-old, so every weekend I would go and stay with my nan and grandad. My grandad was the most gentle kindest man I ever met. His energy was so soft and beautiful, and he called me his Babs until I was well into my twenties. I adored him.

Our weekends were filled with car boot sales where me and my nan would go looking for treasures. My nan taught me how to look for antiques and hallmarked jewellery. We would get there early, and I used to wiggle my way through the crowds of people and go to the front, straight to the old cake tins that people would have filled with bric-a-brac and old necklaces they couldn't be bothered to untangle so they would just throw them away.

I found a platinum diamond necklace once, and the lady gave it me for 75p. I was like a little magpie.

This all sounds like lots of fun, but every Saturday morning before we were due to leave my nan would absolutely tear strips off me for some reason or another, and no matter how much I said sorry for things I hadn't even done she was never happy until I was crying.

I can remember my grandad stepping in one day and shouting, "That's enough June! Are you happy now she's crying? Leave her alone for God's sake, look at her!" And I was sitting on the couch, head bowed down, hugging my toy dog crying my little 6-year-old eyes out while she stood over me, crouched down slightly pointing in my face and screaming at me.

This would happen every weekend and yet I would always go back because after this had happened, she would say she was sorry, and hug me and then we would go out all day and she would buy me lots of things from the car boot sales and take me to the arcades and buy me sweets.

I always tried to make her happy by being really good so she wouldn't do it. But she always did, she would always find something to blame me for. It was like her little kick. This was where my people pleasing began, right there in a place where I was supposed to feel safe and protected. I started saying sorry a lot for things that hadn't happened or things that I thought might make her shout.

Our people pleasing tendencies first develop as a form of self-protection and since I was in constant fear of disapproval and was being criticised for everything, I learnt at a very early age how to give her what she wanted to avoid the rath of her disappointment.

This turned into a vicious cycle of over-giving and overanalysing that played out throughout my life.

2

I FUCKING HATE BULLIES

From having a bully at home and being constantly nervous and submissive, it was pretty much guaranteed that I was going to be targeted in school.

And I was.

I went to a local school not far from where we lived and from as long as I can remember I was bullied. I don't think there was ever a period when I wasn't a target. It was by this one girl, who I can now say with a happy heart that I have forgiven, because I carried this for years and know how poisonous it tastes.

There is a brilliant famous quote by the late Nelson Mandela, he said, *"Holding on to anger is like drinking poison and waiting for the other person to die."*

I was bullied by a popular girl in school, she was always making jokes and making people laugh and all the boys fancied her too. And when you're little this is like a big deal right?

She was the baby in her family and absolutely spoilt rotten. She singled me out and was just unbelievably mean to me. Making nasty comments about my clothes and my face and how I laughed or ate my lunch. Telling other people not to be my friend and making up stories about me.

I can remember one time we had been given homework over the weekend to do with our parents and it was to make our family tree. I was a real arty kid and loved anything like this, so had spent ages doing it. It was so beautiful, I had drawn a big tree and each of the branches was someone in my family's name written on like calligraphy curly writing and pretty autumn coloured leaves on the end.

It was on real thick earthy, textured paper and I was proper proud.

For some reason me and this girl had been seated next to each other even though the teacher knew I was being bullied.

When the teacher asked us to get out our homework, she saw mine and asked to look at it. I just went cold and froze. I really did not want her to touch it.

I said, "No" at first and she said, "WHY NOT? I won't rip it or anything!" She looked angry and everyone was staring at me, so I just gave it to her.

I should have known then what she was going to do.

She slipped the paper out of the plastic wallet, and I just watched in sheer terror as the wallet was just left to fall on the floor.

She held up the paper at the top by each corner and took her time looking over it.

Then I noticed the paper was becoming taught, she was pulling her hands away from each other slowly, so I didn't notice but with force.

Before I could say anything there was a piercing little crack, and a tear appeared right in the middle of the paper.

"Ooops!" she said, "I've ripped it. Sorry!" she was sniggering to the girl next to her and they both began laughing at what she had done.

I could feel hot tears instantly bulging in my eyes! The rage just accelerated through my body, and I started to shake.

But I just sat there. Frozen. Hurt. Embarrassed. And so fuckin angry!

"Awwwww, don't cry!" she said still laughing.

So I didn't. I sucked it all up.

As the class went on, I couldn't concentrate and I began to feel sick. I told the teacher I felt unwell. I didn't even tell off her for ripping my picture. I just wanted it to go away.

The teacher sat me at her desk and all I could see was the back of the bully's head. Her ponytail swinged side to side as she laughed with the other girls, and she kept turning around and smirking at me.

I was still raging. I think this was the angriest I had ever been in my eight little years on the planet.

I kept visualising standing up from my chair, walking over to her really quickly so the teacher couldn't stop me and YANKING her backwards off the chair by her ponytail. Then as she was on the floor, I would straddle her long skinny body and punch the shit out of her face.

And it felt fucking amazing.

But I just couldn't bring myself to do it!

I know my whole life would have been different from that moment if I had done that. But I didn't. And I know it's because life had far more planned for me to endure and learn from.

And so the bullying continued.

3

MAKE UP IN THE KITCHEN

When I was eleven things started getting a bit tense in the house I lived in with my parents.

My mum was going out a lot in the evening on her own. She would get ready while my dad was out playing squash and then when he came in about 8.30pm she would go out and I would just go up and be in my bedroom.

I was never very close to my dad when I was a kid, but that eventually changed as I got older. He is now a massive part of my life.

I remember my mum always had Whitney Houston's 'I will always love you' playing while she was putting her makeup on. Whenever I hear that song now, I can see my mum about 34 years old putting her mascara on in a big wooden mirror in our kitchen that had cherries on the wallpaper. I would watch in amazement as she put on her mascara, and it would make her shiny brown eyes literally triple in size and pop out of her face. She was so beautiful.

On one of these evenings, she put makeup on me for the very first time. I had not long started high school and she told me I was old enough to wear a little bit now. I was quite nervous. She started by putting a bit of bronzer on me first and made my little white cheeks all sun kissed. It was like magic! Then she showed me how to put mascara on. She said it was the one thing she couldn't live without.

She showed me how to open my mouth and make my eyes wide, (I bet you are doing that face right now? Go on admit it). We were both laughing at how silly our faces looked and I couldn't do it for laughing because I was scared I would poke my eye with the brush.

I remember the first time I put it on I could not believe the difference. I looked like a completely different person. It made me feel like I was officially a teenager now I could wear make-up, I was proper buzzing my little boobies off.

I went to school the next day with makeup on just like she had showed me, and I can remember one of my friends coming up to me and saying, "Wow you look so different!" I was so happy!

I knew my mum wasn't happy though, I could tell by just how she was in herself. And she was drinking quite a lot too and her friends were coming round for cups of tea but us kids had to leave the room so the adults could talk.

When I was thirteen my parents split up.

Me and my little brother moved out with my mum into our own house about ten minutes drive from where we lived.

And EVERYTHING changed.

4

THE TOXIC BOYFRIEND

When we moved into our new rented house, we didn't have much. We had some bedroom furniture a TV and our clothes.

I can remember the couch we had in the front room was an old single bed for the first twelve months when we moved in, until one of my friends parents gave us their old three piece suite. My mum just didn't have the money to buy one at the time and we were soooooo grateful when we got a REAL one.

My mum learnt how to wallpaper and saved up enough to decorate the front room. I felt really cosy once it was all done and she was so proud of herself.

Pretty much as soon as we moved into our new house my mum introduced us to a new boyfriend who she had met in work. He was younger than she was by about ten years I think and he had three kids from a previous relationship.

I instantly did not like him. He was cocky, overconfident, rude, crude and unpredictable. He thought he was the dog's bollocks.

I have had to pause here for a minute while writing this, because I just realised how much trauma this man caused to all our lives.

He was toxic on so many levels.

I was thirteen at the time and going through a bit of a difficult time in high school. I can remember coming in from school one day really upset and wanting to speak to my mum.

They were both in the kitchen when I got in and I went to see her crying my eyes out. I asked to speak to my mum in private but wouldn't leave the room.

My mum tried to make him but instead he picked her up, threw her over his shoulder, carried her upstairs and had sex with her really, really loudly.

Me and my brother who was nine at the time didn't know what to do, so we just sat downstairs in the living room. Shocked at what was happening we just turned up the TV until it was all over.

I felt like I wasn't important anymore at that moment.

But this was only the start.

5

GET THE FUCK OFF MY MUM

Money was very tight in our house at this time, and it became very clear that if I wanted nice things like new clothes or trainers or makeup etc, that I would have to get a job myself to get them. All the morning my mum had was paying for the house and the bills and the food.

So, by the time I was 15 I had four jobs, I worked in a chippy, hairdressers, a restaurant and a newsagent. I did these in the evenings after school and at weekends. This meant I never have to ask for anything which was good because she couldn't have afforded to get me anything even though she wanted to.

The toxic boyfriend had also moved in by now, and every week his three kids would come and stay. They were little shites.

His kids would just fight and cause mayhem in the house. They were all under eight years, the youngest was about three. I used to dread them coming. There was no spare room for them to go in so it would always be a big drama at bedtime where everyone would have to find a space to sleep.

Another thing that started happening between my mum and the boyfriend was quite frequent explosive and often violent arguments.

There had never been any sort of violence in our lives before. Even when my mum and dad would argue, the most violent thing that ever happened was my dad stormed out the room after an argument and my mum threw a wooden spoon at the back of his head. Luckily, she missed and it went flying past him.

My mum was a strong-minded woman. Even though my nan had pretty much stripped her of any independence as she was growing up, as our mother, she was fierce.

The arguments would come out of nowhere.

He would react aggressively to pretty much anything my mum said and would get right in her face and begin manhandling her. He did all this in front of those kids. He did not care.

I would try and tell him to stop, and he would scream me down, telling me it was, "None of my fucking business!" and to, "Get out the room now!".

I would never go because I was scared what he would do.

One time he broke her fingers, and another time he burst her ear drum. Not to mention all the bruises and the scratches and the tears.

He broke my mum's heart.

One night I was sleeping and was woken up by what I thought was a car alarm going off. I lay there confused for a minute then realised it was my mum screaming my name. I shot out of bed and ran into her bedroom.

She was face down on the floor at the side of the bed, and he was straddled over her sitting on the back of her neck. I grabbed the wooden truncheon my mum kept at the side of her bed and screamed, "Get the fuck off my mum NOW!"

He could see I was serious, so he got off.

I helped my mum up and she was shaking and sobbing. I wanted to call the police, but she told me not to.

He wouldn't leave the room. And my mum told me to go back to bed. The next day she told me she asked him to leave but he wouldn't and that's why it happened.

This continued to happen frequently over the next few years as she tried to get him to leave, but he just refused to go.

And slowly but surely, we just had to sit and watch as he was destroying our mum.

6

SAVED BY A BEEP!

I was very self-sufficient as a teenager. My mum wasn't very present, as she had her own shit going on, and she had changed so much because of this bad relationship with the boyfriend.

One day she was in work, and I was getting ready to go out and meet my boyfriend.

He was in her bedroom, and he called me in. I went in and he told me that we never spend any time together so to come and give him a quick hug him on the bed. I said, "No thanks!" and I turned to leave, but he made out he just wanted a cuddle.

Looking back, I should have just said no and left, but the nervous people pleaser in me gave me no choice. So, I went and sat next to him on the bed. He put his arm around me and started to hug me. Then ask me a question I will never forget. He leant into my ear and said, "Your mum said you have big nipples like her is that true?"

I couldn't believe my ears!

I froze with fear as he snuggled into me more. The next thing there was a loud beep and my boyfriend had come to pick me up.

I leapt off the bed. "Got to go, bye!" I said and ran down the stairs as fast as I could.

As I was leaving the house, he shouted for me not to tell my mum because she would never believe me.

So I didn't tell her for years.

Someone was watching over me that day because had that been a few minutes later who knows what could have happened. I told my boyfriend and he wanted to come in to confront him but I wouldn't let him.

I'm so grateful that what could have been something quite awful never got to happen.

Finally, when I was about seventeen, he left.

The only reason he left was because he got caught cheating, which my mum had suspected for years. He had suspicious looking love bites which were apparently bruises from football and was going out more with his mates and staying out all night. Then would accuse my mum of cheating all the time and became very possessive.

One day a woman called Bev rang and told my mum they had been together in a relationship for over a year, he had told her my mum was so sick with cancer that he couldn't leave her. But he has started getting aggressive, so she found my mum's number and decided she would have a bit of revenge.

I am to this day so fucking grateful for this woman.

God love her, he probably beat the shit out of her for doing what she did, but she saved my mum's life.

He went on to his next victim very quickly, a woman my mum worked with who looked a lot like her.

She regularly came into work with black eyes and bruises. I know this was a bad thing to think and I used to feel sorry for the woman, but I was just so glad it wasn't my mum anymore.

7

THE DICTATOR

Of all the chapters in this book the next few will be the ones filled with the most darkness for me. This is the story of where I went from a free spirited sparkly little butterfly, to becoming a nervous, timid, lost soul who was scared of her own shadow.

Looking back at how I even allowed this to happen makes my heart hurt.

I stayed for so long even though I was dying inside because I wanted so much for him to just love me.

I met him when I was nineteen and had started work as a civil servant. He was twenty-four. At first, he was kind and complimented me all the time. He showed me off to all his friends and bought me lots of gifts. Like all the time.

We got married when I was tweny-one, (and I left, or escaped rather when I was twenty-five).

I should have noticed all the signs that people were pointing out to me from the very beginning that something wasn't right, but I just didn't want to see them.

He didn't like any of my friends was the first alarm bell that went off. In the end my closest most bestest friend throughout my school life backed off because she couldn't stand to see what was happening to me.

I was partying every weekend with him and all of his friends, and because that wasn't her thing, plus he was twisting everything she said to make out she was judging me, we lost contact.

I also had a good male friend I had known for years. I had gone to his mums 50th party as I had known the family for years and I got accused of sleeping with him. Everything I said he twisted and made out I was lying, so I stopped seeing him too.

He also didn't like my mum.

Now this should have sent me running straight for the hills because EVERYBODY liked my mum.

But I loved him. And I didn't want to lose him. And he made it unbelievably difficult for me to take my mum's side when he was slagging her off and making out that she was the bad guy. Again, he twisted everything she said to mean the worst possible scenario. He even accused her of lying and withholding money from us when we were getting a mortgage, saying she had said she would give us some money towards a deposit. She had never said this.

I was in so much pain. And my mum could see this.

She didn't back down to him, but she could see I was caught in the middle, so she also stepped away. Not wanting me to be in any more turmoil than I already was. This right here was unconditional love.

Everything was always about his family and his friends, and if there was ever anything going on with my work or my family, he would make excuses and I would always end up going alone.

But while I was out, he would be messaging me asking me when I was home, or he would cause a big row before I went out so that I wouldn't end up going.

Another thing that should have been a HUGE sign was that he wasn't affectionate.

At all.

Like zero hugs.

For anyone that knows me knows that I am one of the biggest huggers EVERRRRRR!

If I ever went to give him a hug, he would cold hug me quickly, or just refuse saying that I had had one earlier.

When I eventually tried to leave him the first time and gave this as one of my reasons, he told me that I should go to the doctors because it was me who had the problems and I had emotional issues wanting attention all the time.

Another thing that he liked to do was while we were out with friends in the pub and I was talking to someone, he would come right over, stand next to the person I was talking to and say to me, "Were leaving NOW!" and walk out of the pub.

The person who I was talking to would just be like, "What the hell is the matter with him?" and I would be so embarrassed that

I would just apologise and grab my things and scurry out the door after him.

I would often have to run to catch him up, shouting his name as he ignored me and carried on marching away. Then when I did catch up and asked him what was wrong, he would reply with, "You know what you've done!"

I didn't. I had no idea.

And he wouldn't tell me or either, sometimes he wouldn't speak to me for days. Completely blanking me when I spoke to him or even sat next to him crying saying I was sorry for the things I had done. Even though I didn't even know what they were.

I just wanted things to be better and to feel like he loved me.

I know now that this is emotional abuse.

And this is actually a thing.

Unlike my emotional issues of wanting to be hugged, that is not actually a thing. That's normal for humans to want to be hugged.

Non-Narcissistic humans anyway.

I wish I could go back to younger me and give her a shake. Tell her that she doesn't need to put up with that abuse and she should leave.

But even if that was possible, I still wouldn't have listened. I was lost and in far too deep.

8

DON'T YOU TAKE THAT FUCKING MEDICINE!

I always wanted to have children for as long as I can remember. Even in my teens I would sabotage my pill and miss a couple of days to see what would happen! I cannot believe I did that now.

Looking back now, I'm bloody glad that I never got caught out when I was younger but at the time it felt so exciting and I was really broody, it felt like a deep inner craving that I couldn't silence. A few of my friends in school got pregnant and I secretly felt a bit jealous. I used to puff out my belly, arch my back and then rub my belly pretending there was a baby in there.

All the women in my family had a baby girl when they were twenty-three years old. My mum, my nan, my great nan, her mum, so to me this was just a given that when ***I*** was twenty-three, I would have my little girl too.

But this never happened.

I started trying for a baby when I was twenty-one with the dictator -sneakily before but never got caught - so after about twelve months and no joy we got referred for tests and I ended up having to have an operation to see why we weren't conceiving.

It's easy for men, all they have to do is have a little fiddle, collect the prize in a little jar and bob's your uncle.

Us women have to endure the whole pot holing experience, with all sorts of special probing and prodding instruments. Then there is the whole chit chat bollocks, "Are you going on holiday?" "Where do you work?" And all you really want to say is, "Can you not speak to me while you have your head inside my vagina please love, I can't concentrate properly."

Laid there imagining Tom Hardy or whoever floats your boat having a good old rummage instead of some awkward Doctor with rubber gloves and a plastic apron on.

I had the operation, it was a laparoscopy and a hysteroscopy. It was just a day case, and I was in recovery eating my toast and tea feeling absolutely off my tits still on morphine, when the nurse passed by and decided to just casually mention that results had shown I might never be able to have children.

Can you imagine one minute being in a purple fuzzy haze of morphine hugs, with a gob full of the bestest jammy toast you have ever had, minding your own business and then BANG! Someone's words have the same effect as a big kick in the fanny and your whole world feels like it has been blown apart.

This sent me spiralling very quickly into a deep and much darker depression than I had ever thought possible. I felt like I was broken. I felt like I was not good enough and I felt like what was the point to my life if I couldn't have children? As in that was something I had longed for practically my whole life so what now? Not to mention living with a partner who was also depressed and on medication and the pair of us numbing ourselves by self-medicating every weekend.

My mum took me on a girl's holiday to cheer me up, a week away just me and her and her crazy but super big-hearted friend. We did have a good time, and she would say to me every day, "It's all going to be okay you know babes, it'll work itself out." Our friends and family were really supportive too and the dictator talked about it constantly to people saying that we probably will need IVF and how hard it was going to be for us.

It took six months for the consultant's appointment to come through, in which time I was now also on medication for my depression. We went to the appointment expecting news of my infertility and to be referred to the IVF waiting list or something and I almost fell off my chair when they told us the results.

I had twisted fallopian tubes on the left side, which was very common and could mean that sometimes I didn't ovulate. The dictator had sperm that swam extremely slow, so this could cause a problem but not to worry for now. They prescribed us a drug called clomid which meant I would ovulate loads more eggs and we would have a much higher chance of conceiving naturally.

I was GOB SMACKED! He looked even more shocked. Scared almost. We told them about what the nurse had said about me not being able to have children and they apologised, but I didn't care anymore. This news was even better to me than winning the lottery!

I burst into tears I was so happy and just couldn't control myself. He just stared at me, like he wasn't really present and was processing everything in his head.

I burst out of the consultant's office with the prescription tightly in my hand like it was the most precious thing in the world. Like Charlie when he found the golden ticket in Charlie and the Chocolate Factory. I was SO FUCKIN EXCITED! I reckon that was the first time I ever found out I could pee glitter!

On the way down the corridor, I chattered away excitedly about the news and our plans and how amazing it was and then he cut me off mid-sentence and said, "Don't you fuckin take that!"

I stopped skipping and felt his dark energy consume me like a heavy wet blanket. "What do you mean?" I said completely confused.

"Don't you take that fuckin medicine!" he said. He stopped and pointed his finger right in my face and glared into my eyes, " If I find out you have fuckin taken it I will leave you! Do you hear me! I am NOT ready to have a baby!" And he carried on walking down the corridor.

Leaving me just standing there in pure disbelief. Crushed to the point I instantly had hot fat tears streaming down my face. That was the day he chipped a piece of my heart away.

9

A LITTLE BIT OF HAPPY

As my nan used to say, "I don't want to bore the tit ends off you..." (I love this) so I will fast forward a few years.

We all escaped from the toxic boyfriend, my mum went on holiday to Egypt and met the love of her life, sold her house and went to live in the beautiful sunshine. FINALLY she was happy! It was about bloody time bless her gorgeous heart. She had met her soul mate. Even though he was 20 years younger he ADORED her, and their souls instantly recognised each other.

I also eventually escaped from the dictator. Yayyyyyyy!

One day while I was working in the bank, a handsome man with a huge smile and sparkly sexy energy came into my office, his name was Mikey.

We instantly connected. It was like something I had never felt before. I felt like I had known him my whole life and he made me feel so comfortable and safe. Like I could really relax and be myself around him. Something I wasn't used to feeling at home. We swapped numbers.

Not long after I went on holiday to see my mum, I went alone as the dictator didn't want to come, because why did he want to see my mum? It was my mum not his?

So, I went with my brother.

While I was away, I would ring him to see how he was, but he was always too busy to talk to me, or would say he didn't have anything to say. He had no interest in anything I was doing.

Meanwhile, Mikey was texting me and chatting away to me constantly, he even rang me to see how I was getting on and was I having a nice time.

And then one night he sent me a message that said, "I can't stop thinking about you. You are the first thing I think of in the morning and the last thing I think of when I go to bed."

And my heart just *knew*.

I couldn't stay any longer where I was unhappy.

When we returned home, I tried to leave the dictator and was told everything was okay, it was me who had emotional issues and also that he now wanted to have a baby so that I should get a prescription for that medication so we could start trying straight away...I had no words.

Well, I did... Goodbye.

In between this happening, I had been to see a psychic, who told me that I my marriage was over so I should take off my ring, and that I hadn't had a baby girl at twenty-three because I was with the wrong man. And I would have her, but I would have a boy first. Also, I was going to be with a man with the initial M and he was going to love me more than I could ever know.

(This all came true)

When I left the dictator, he told all of my friends that I had been cheating on him, and made up a story I was pregnant with another man's baby and had gone to Egypt to have an abortion. So all of our friends stopped speaking to me. He also told me he had hired a private investigator and had had me followed so he knew everything that I was doing.

Leaving him was the best decision I ever made.

And I never wished him anything other than to be happy, but I knew that was never going to be with me.

About eighteen months after being together with Mikey, I found out I was pregnant with our son Nathan. He was my little miracle baby after all the problems I had had before, and his name means *Gift from God.*

We got married when Nathan was five months old and four years later were gifted our baby girl Daisy-Louise.

Mikey already had a son also called Mikey from a previous relationship, so our house was now happy and full.

Although this was all amazing and I was more loved and happier than I had ever been, I was still drinking and self-medicating every weekend because it was not yet time for my healing journey to begin.

10

STEP FORWARD ANXIETY, DEPRESSION AND PANIC ATTACKS

For so long I had used drink to escape from anything that didn't feel like fun.

I also felt I couldn't have fun unless I had to drink.

From the age of about fourteen I had got drunk pretty much every weekend, apart from when I was having my children. Drink had always been a huge part of my life.

But what happened was, even though I had the children my life didn't change. Here is where mum guilt steps in. I would get the kids to bed and have a drink like most people do. Except I would sometimes still be awake in the morning when they woke up. This made me feel like shit. I would then shame myself for being a bad mother and feel guilty, on top of having the mother of all hangovers. But it still didn't make me stop.

I would feel so bad during the week any coping mechanisms I had were nowhere to be seen and I had no energy for myself never mind the kids and work in the house.

So come Friday I was ready for my stress release. My bottle of vodka.

And the whole sequence would start again. My hangovers as I got older had also started lasting longer and becoming more and more unkind. It was a vicious cycle. One I tried to break time and time again, but it was just so hard.

My main circle of family and friends were big drinkers, and this had been my routine for years, so when I tried to stop and step away, they made me feel like I was being a weirdo. Or would say, "That's OK, it'll make you feel better. Just have one!"

I didn't want to offend anyone by not drinking, so it was easier to just play along. As the saying goes, too much of anything is never a good thing. Please step forward Anxiety, depression, and daily panic attacks.

The trouble here was the thing that was causing all these monstrosities within me was also the one thing that could make them disappear after just one drink.

I was caught in a trap.

A self-inflicted trap.

But something had to change

After Nathan was born in 2008, I was doing really well and was hardly drinking at all. Then one sunny Tuesday morning in 2010, I was in an armed robbery in work. Three men wearing balaclavas armed with machetes and wrecking bars stormed in and terrorised the bank.

The attack was less than ninety seconds long but it felt like everything happened in slow motion. I ended up with PTSD and what I think was delayed post-natal depression showed its ugly little face too.

I remember sitting on the edge of the bed just sobbing one night, I was so lost.

My anxiety was through the roof, and I was an absolute nervous wreck. My mum was in Egypt at the time and we spoke at least once a week on the phone, but I missed her so much.

I went on antidepressants for a while, but they made me feel completely numb. It was better than how I was feeling though, and they got me through a really dark phase. But even though I was told not to on the tablets, I was still drinking. Except now I didn't feel like shit because of the medication, so I could do it more.

I came off them after about nine months and was pretty much in the same position as when I had gone on them, just a bit fatter, as a side effect of the tablets, was not giving a shit so I was eating everything in sight.

Fast forward a few years after Daisy was born and I was even worse. I thought having my baby girl would have made everything peachy, she was the cherry on our cake. But the truth was I had never dealt with anything.

Ever.

The bullying.

The narcissism.

The bank raid.

The addictions.

By now my panic attacks were every day and I couldn't leave the house without someone with me. Luckily my mum had moved back from Egypt by then, so she was with me a lot.

At this time, I felt like I had no control over anything in my life, but the one thing I could control was what I ate. I developed some very unusual eating habits. I forbid myself from eating certain foods I believed to be unhealthy or fattening and I was obsessed with what I weighed. I now know this is called Orthorexia.

I thought I looked great, but on the inside, I was so unbelievably sad; the lack of food and the obsessive control I had over everything was triggering my anxiety and panic attacks.

Although I was eating lots of healthy food, it just wasn't enough for what my body needed. I needed a good pie is what my mum kept telling me. And she was right, but at the time the thought of eating that pastry and what it would do to my body and how many calories it had would almost tip me over the edge.

Even my drinking was vodka which is pure, and sugar free mixers. I was neurotic.

My mum was so good, she could see I was unwell and was there for me but without making me feel like I was a mess.

And I was almost at rock bottom.

This is where my healing journey began.

I discovered Reiki first, which I will share with you in more detail very soon.

A little while after I found yoga.

I believe that yoga helped me to get sober. (ha, that rhymes!)

The breathing techniques and gentle movements massively helped my anxiety and within a few weeks I wasn't having panic attacks anymore. A few weeks later I had unintentionally come off my anxiety medication because I felt so good, I had forgotten to take it.

The difference in me was immeasurable and I knew that if it had helped me that it could help other women who were going through what I was too.

In 2017 I trained to become a yoga teacher. Now more than ever I wanted to stop drinking and I was able to put on yoga classes to stop me from doing this.

I would put a class on Friday nights, Saturday mornings and Sunday mornings too so that when people invited me for a drink I could say, "I can't I'm working," and they wouldn't question it at all. It wasn't easy let me tell you. I would come home from yoga on Friday night to Mikey and a few of our friends drinking in the kitchen, and it was so tempting, but I knew that I wanted to do it.

It takes twenty-one days to make or break a new habit and this felt like walking through treacle. It was heavy going, all my demons came out, my inner bitch piped up and everyone's smart comments like, "Ooooh get you not drinking again, you're good aren't you!" really pissed me off.

Me not drinking triggered a lot of people at first. Sometimes people are triggered because we are doing something that they really want to do as well, but just aren't ready or don't have the willpower to do it. To them this makes it look like we think we are better than they are, and they get all defensive or make fun of you. But that is not the truth.

What I found about not drinking, is it became a lot easier when I told myself I could if I wanted too rather than I can't.

If you are anything like me if someone tells me I can't, I'm fucking DEFINITELY doing it!

By saying I don't want to rather than I can't, I was able to tell myself that I was in control, and I was choosing not to do it. It became my choice, and it felt so much lighter and less restricted and a decision that I knew was true and right for me.

How we talk to ourselves really does make a massive difference. I will be talking a lot more about this very soon.

11

AND JUST LIKE THAT THEY WERE GONE

Fast forward a few years to my mid-thirties.

I got a call one evening from my biological dad's partner saying that he was very ill. Over the years I had kept in touch with him, as he and my mum never separated on bad terms. I had even been over to see him where he lived in Germany a few times over the years.

He had been in hospital for over 9 months with what they could only describe as an autoimmune disease and even after a liver transplant he wasn't getting any better.

I instantly booked a flight and went over two weeks later.

Shocked is an understatement.

When I saw him, he looked like a fragile old man. All of his hair had fallen out, he was swollen and was hooked up to different types of machines. He was so happy to see me, and although he had just had a tracheostomy a few days before he managed to find enough strength to speak to me.

It was devastating, seeing this man who had once been a famous musician and the life and soul of the party, now so fragile and consumed by pain.

The last day I was there he was in so much pain. He was in and out of consciousness all day. He opened his eyes at one point and saw me and mouthed, “I love you.” to me.

A week later he passed away.

Losing a parent is such a powerful feeling. This sounds really obvious, but this isn’t what I mean. For me it was like a massive part of me had been lost, and that I had a little bit of emptiness inside that I couldn’t quite explain. The pain was unbelievable.

I remember thinking if I felt like this about him dying, and we weren’t that close, then how was I going to feel if I lost my mum.

I actually said this to my mum at the time too. She was back living in the UK by this time thankfully and we were closer than we had ever been.

One day as I was leaving the house my mum pulled up in her car, she got out looking shell shocked and just sat on my front garden wall unable to speak. She put her head in her hands and began to cry!

“WHAT’S HAPPENED?” I kept asking her, but she couldn’t speak for ages. Then she told me she has been for a chest x-ray for the cough that she had and they had found shadows and pockets of infection on her left lung.

My mum had developed this weird cough that wouldn’t go away. She was waking up with water in the back of her throat and was coughing up water too. She also had pain in her shoulder and across her back, so after a few months of toing and froing from the Doctor's she got an x-ray.

After numerous tests and investigations, she was diagnosed with terminal lung cancer.

Just six months after my biological dad Les had died.

I remember looking up at the sky and shouting, "Are you fucking kidding me!!"

How could this be happening? First my biological dad and now my mum; this was like a bad dream.

I can remember the day of her diagnosis.

It was just me and her in the consultant's room, and there was a Macmillan nurse in there too, so I guessed it wasn't going to be good news. I wore my favourite top with flowers on and lucky daisy earrings. I had been praying to whoever was listening for positive results, but you could tell by the energy in the room that we were about to have our hearts shattered.

The consultant introduced herself and said the results of the tests had come back and it was confirmed that she had stage four terminal lung cancer.

We just looked at each other and the whole room began to spin. I went cold and I felt my heart drop.

This couldn't be happening.

But it was.

My mum just stared at me open mouthed, her eyes looked vacant, and I could see her head had gone. I tried to listen as best

I could to what the consultant was explaining but none of it was going in.

The Macmillan nurse gave us some handouts and confirmed mum's next appointment, but she was completely in shock at this point. She was just staring at me wide eyed like, 'what just happened?'

We walked outside the hospital towards the car in silence not believing what we had just been told. We found a corridor with nobody around and we hugged and sobbed in each other's arms. (I'm crying writing this).

We didn't care how much noise we made it all just came out.

There were just no words.

Her journey through this was one of total strength and courage. When her immunotherapy treatment stopped responding, she tried chemotherapy. Within twenty-four hours of her first infusion, she was in A&E bleeding from her bowel. After this, she decided to surrender and not continue with any chemotherapy, as it was spreading very quickly, and she wanted quality of life over the slim possibility of quantity.

I remember while she was still at home one day, she told me to come and sit down with her on the bed. She took my hand and told me not to be sad about what was happening, because this was what was supposed to happen because it was her journey in life and that she had had an amazing life, full of love and happy memories and she was okay with it all. She had surrendered and made peace.

I was a crying my eyes out sitting next to her.

This was definitely not fucking okay AT ALL!

But by her saying this, and her having no resistance to dying, even though she knew death was pretty much waiting around the corner for her, made it a bit easier for us too.

I remember thinking, "You are my fucking hero!"

She then told me to pass her the jewellery box because she wanted to give me her jewellery now, not someone do it after she had gone, and for me to pick what I wanted.

This absolutely broke me in half.

She wasn't having no for an answer though. It was one of the most emotional moments of my whole life.

Twelve months after her diagnosis my mum passed away.

This was the catalyst that made me change my whole life.

12

THE DAY I LOST DORIS

Something happened to me the day my mum died.

I realised that it was just me now, and from that moment on I only had myself to rely on. My mum had been by mostest bestest friend in the whole world. The bond we had was unbreakable. We used to talk for hours on the phone about absolutely nothing and had the same stupid sense of humour. We were as they say, two peas in a pod.

We even sounded the same when we spoke. If I ever answered the phone while she was driving or something her friends used to say, "Hiya Jan love...." And just start waffling away to me. She was my go-to for everything. I could tell her anything and she would never judge me or tell me off or make me feel stupid or shitty.

She would always lend me money or buy me things I needed if I was a bit skint and would have given me her last penny.

She adored me.

I was her shining star, and she was my Doris.

Her real name was Jan, but she got the name Doris one day when we were shopping at Asda. She was at the till and I was packing her bags for her. The cashier told her the price and she was taking an extra-long time to work out her money. She was struggling a bit to figure it out and she looked at the cashier like she had ten heads, then she looked at me, then she looked at the cashier, and then the cashier gave me a look, like, "Can you help her?"

I said joking, "It's ok, I'm her carer, come on Doris, let's sort you out there love.".

"You cheeky bitch!" she said half laughing half wanting to poke me in the face. And from that moment on, she was my Doris.

I lost my mum on the 16th of July 2018. I say my mum, but really, I should be saying our mum as I also have a younger brother, but she was also mum to about fifty other people she has tucked under her bosom along the way.

If you ask anyone what they remember about my mum its was that she gave the best hugs, and you could go to her with ANYTHING. She was just so full of love and kindness. Everyone adored her, and my friends always used to say, "I wish my mum was like your mum!" She just had such a gorgeous big heart.

Losing her was the catalyst that made me change completely.

It made me realise that life is so unpredictable, you just do not know what is lurking around the corner. I hope I'm not coming across as being morbid, but it made me realise that if my life was ever going to change then it was ONLY ME who could make it happen.

And the clock was ticking. It has taken me thirty-eight years to realise this!

It was time to take shit seriously now.

13

WE ARE ALL MADE OF STARS

I really wanted to share with you all the dark stuff first to show you that I am human just like you, and that some really shitty, horrible things have happened to me too.

These things eventually made me wake the fuck up and realise that life was not going to wait for me until I was ready.

Life just keeps happening around us, and if we don't start moving our beautiful asses and actually start doing the things we talk about, then we might just miss the bus of our dreams.

When I was standing in the room at the hospice looking at my mum after she had just passed away, I remember thinking, "Shit! Did that just happen?"

Twelve months ago, we had been planning our big family holiday to Lanzarote and talking about how she wanted to go to the Maldives with her husband but didn't know which Island. And now she couldn't do any of that.

It made me realise that if anyone was going to make changes in my life, then it was going to have to be me. My mum was the person I went to first with all my worries and my problems and for advice. She was my rock. She always made everything better and no matter what it was I knew that by telling her that I was going to be ok.

Now it was on me. From that moment, I gave myself permission to do the things that I had dreamed of doing NOW. Start putting plans in place now to make them happen because who knows what tomorrow brings? (Is that a song? I bet you just sung it in your head!)

And the moment I REALISED that I had a choice, and that I was the only one who could make any changes in my life and accepted that life sometimes liked to shout, "CATCH!" and throw you a hot fresh turd, this lit the biggest fire under my arse EVERRRRRRR!!

The start of my healing journey was not a planned thing, but then I don't think it really is for anyone. I think for everyone something BIG normally happens to them or they subconsciously stumble upon it at the perfect time.

Since I was a little girl, I had always loved anything to do with the thought of there being something bigger than us. Something that made us all be the same and all connected. I loved anything to do with spirituality, crystals, unexplained coincidences, aliens, and everything that was a little bit woo woo and different.

But throughout my life I had been told by certain people that it was weird. That it was all a load of bollocks and not true and a waste of time. It almost felt like it was a bit forbidden or wrong.

I always felt there was a calling inside of me, and the more I listened to it and followed it, the more I felt myself light up inside. Like it was something I recognised or had always known.

I want to share something with you before we go any further with this journey together because I remember how I felt when I first started, and I wish someone had said it to me.

It is so important that you listen to this voice inside of you and follow your own path and shine your own sparkly gorgeous light into the world in your own way. YOUR version. Always be true to what feels right for you. It is okay to be the *weirdo* that like the hippy dippy spiritual stuff if that's what makes YOU happy.

When I found the courage to listen to and follow the calling of the deep desires that came from within me somewhere and the unexplainable excited feelings in my belly to discover the things that really lit me up, I realised that this was my reason for being here. To help other women in the world to do the same. By sharing my story and my experiences and the things that I have learned I could inspire and ignite the souls of others to do the same.

To feel the gratitude and connection and just pure fucking love of life that I now have.

I have now stopped looking outside for validation and approval from other people. I have stopped comparing myself to people as much as I used to, and when this does happen now, I am able to notice this happening and take a step back, nurture myself and reconnect into my self-awareness.

I have stopped doubting myself when making important decisions, using my intuition and energy to guide me.

I have allowed myself to be ME!

And right here, right now, I am handing you a virtual permission slip that allows you to do the same.

For you to be YOU.

Maybe for the first time in your whole life, be YOU!

And if you don't yet know what that looks like PLEASE DO NOT PANIC. I didn't either when I first decided to be me. I was like who even am I? I am here to help you feel so empowered and so clear on how YOU feel and what you want that you won't have any choice but to Pee Glitter. I will also help you to uncover the reasons why you have been staying small.

Fear is such a big, complicated bag of self-sabotage and conditioned beliefs, we will be delving into all of this together later in the book.

Sometimes we get unintentionally caught up running along with everyone else in some sort of same direction, thinking that we need to keep up with them and be like them and do all the things that they are doing because they seem to be having the best life. But then it all feels a little heavy and your heart slumps back in your chest and makes you need to take a big breath and for the first time in what seems like forever you slow the fuck down and look around.

You realise that you have been caught up in a bit of a tornado and all the shit you're doing that's supposed to be making you happy is actually draining the life out of your soul.

It's never too late to stop and change direction.

Nevereverevereverever!

You are YOU!

There is only ONE of you on the little spinny planet.

Bit of a gross fact but I fuckin' love it so I am going to share it anyway.

There is a one in a 40'000 trillion quadrillion million chance (might not be exact figures but you get the picture!) that you were the little wriggler (yes the sperm) that made it to being accepted by the egg. Because apparently our little eggs are very fussy about which little wriggler they accept as their chosen one. They don't allow just any wriggler to enter.

We must have had some proper wriggly magic going on right from the get-go!

It is SOOOOOOOOO important that we do the things that make US happy. If we really allow ourselves to HEAR the messages and the little nudges our bodies and souls are giving us and choose the things that make us want to pee glitter then we CANNOT get it wrong!

We just need to TRUST and BELIEVE and CONNECT to ourselves!

The noise of everything outside of us can be proper deafening sometimes. Think about all the stuff going on in the world right now, all the different people's opinions and the fear of this new and totally different space we are slowly being opened up to from the fall out of this global pandemic.

And then there's the people who unintentionally suck the life out of us and infect us with their dark heavy often spikey energy (we all know that person).

If we can step away from this and protect our own energy and notice how WE feel about things instead of being influenced into how we SHOULD feel, or how other people EXPECT us to feel, then life begins to feel aligned and in flow and a bit magic and happy and fun.

And... IT DOES NOT MATTER WHAT YOU DO!

It could be crocheting or singing or writing or dog walking or cooking whatever lights YOU up!

We think we need to be doing BIG things and making BIG money is this life to be successful but think about it, what is the one thing that is most important to most people in life? Being Happy.

Choose what is right for YOU! Listen to YOUR beautiful sparkly heart and do the things that make YOU happy!

Speaking of sparkles, we are all actually made of stars. It's 100% true, nearly all of the elements in the human body were made in a star and many have come through several supernovas.

How AMAZING is that! My mum used to call me her shining star. And I bloody am!

So, let me introduce to the first part of my spiritual journey where I discovered Reiki energy healing and how it changed the way my whole world looked.

14

WHAT THE FUCK IS UNIVERSAL ENERGY?

By the time I was thirty-five my panic attacks were so bad I couldn't leave the house. I also had horrendous bouts of sciatica and my anxiety was off the scale.

At this time, I was self-medicating every weekend because this helped me to forget how shit I felt for a few hours. Then I would be hungover and fuzzy for a few days, and by the time my anxiety had took full control again it was almost the weekend so I could look forward to numbing myself again.

I was working in a bank at the time and was constantly off sick but I didn't care. I just lived for the weekends.

Something desperately needed to change and it was like the universe was watching over me as I spiralled deeper and deeper out of control, just waiting to step in at exactly the right moment.

The start of my healing journey was not planned at all.

I believe now that everything happens for a reason, and I believe I was late taking my son to school on that day so I could bump into an old work colleague.

She added me on Facebook and a few days later I saw she was running a Reiki level 1 attunement course. I had had Reiki sessions when I was younger but never really understood what it was. I felt draw to do it so I rocked up to see what it was all about.

During the workshop, I had no idea what she was going on about. WTF was *universal energy*? I thought I was open minded, but this was like proper hippy dippy crazy shit even for me! But I listened and did the stuff she said and after the attunement I started my homework as I was instructed, and something began to happen.

So, let me just stop here a minute and ask if any of you have ever had Reiki?

Reiki is a hard experience to describe due to its very nature. And because we are all different and perceive things differently and we are all made of different energies, the experience is very different for each of us. Every time we have it it's different because we are different every day depending what shiz we are going through at that time.

Reiki is a form of energy healing that was discovered by Dr Mikao Usui of Japan in the early 20th century. The word REI- means divinely inspired or spiritually guided and KI means universal life force energy.

Reiki is a technique used to transmit or channel this energy to yourself and others. This energy can be felt when we place our hands on ourselves or the other person and it feels AMAZING!

My homework was some reading and to practice Reiki on myself for twenty-one days. This is called a Reiki cleanse and is done at the beginning of our Reiki journey to help us start to feel into our own energy.

During the training I was told how everything is made of energy, even us and that external influences and experiences and lifestyle choices affect our energy. I was still sceptical. But I began to feel different. I began to feel happier and more relaxed and not like I wanted to hide from things anymore.

This shit was crazy to me still, but it was helping me feel better, so I carried on. I did my Level 2 attunement and then my Masters Level 3.

And EVERYTHING changed.

Okay so this next bit might sound a bit mental but go with me.

I felt connected to the universe.

I could now feel and influence my own energies and other people's by using positive intentions and my hands.

It was like magic.

During my training I was having regular Reiki sessions and this was where my healing began. I was able to listen to my body and my body showed me where it needed healing, and I began to feel like I was getting a bit of control back in my life. Like I had a bit of power over what was happening for the first time in my life and could actually control it.

I felt like I BELONGED.

Belonged to something bigger than me, something that so many others were connected to, that I belonged to the universe.

My body was giving me subtle messages and had been my whole life, and when I could understand these and take notice, I was able to re-balance my body and feel centred and in control.

Over the next few chapters I will be introducing you to my transformational 5 Pillar programme: **The Feminine Energy Guide**.

This programme is just EVERYTHING to me, and I adore it with every iddy biddy cell of my being. It is all of the things that have been part of my spiritual awakening and healing journey over the last ten years, and I have had so many mind-blowing and life changing results.

I am going to share with you how spirituality will help you to create clarity, confidence and abundance in your life and business if you have one.

To allow you to make soul guided, heart centred decisions that light you up and make you feel so connected to yourself that you realise that you are exactly where you are supposed to be, and you cannot get this wrong!

I will help you to get to know and understand yourself at a deeper level than ever before, so that you can bring the real you into your everyday life.

Have you always dreamt of doing some of the things that give you butterflies for as long as you can remember, but you don't have the confidence to do it?

I know how this feels because I used to be like this too.

Then I finally thought "Fuck it, life is too short!"

I will help you feel connected on a deeper level than ever before to allow yourself to:

- Create a life filled with purpose and ambition.
- Do the things you've longed to do.
- Become the very best version of you that you can be.
- Use your intuition to make decisions that feel aligned and easy.
- Listen to your inner voice rather than the opinion of other's.
- Feel free to embrace your spirituality and bring this into your life to help you fulfil your dreams.

When I was trying to make decisions about things or get creative, I would find it hard not to look at what other people were doing and instantly compare myself. I would then feel like I wasn't good enough, or who did I think I was, talking about all this stuff like I was an expert? Imposter syndrome would take over and I would talk myself out of doing ANYTHING at all.

When I began to use my energy as my guide, work on my inner bitch mindset and bring in elements of spirituality EVERYTHING began to change and I am so excited to share this with you.

Using all the knowledge I have gathered I am here to help you to connect to your spirituality and embrace who you truly are. I discovered that bringing spirituality into all areas of my life was when the magic happened and that's when everything in life fell into place.

You have the power to create a life that feels so aligned that you really ***can*** bring your dreams to life!

I will be taking you on a journey through my 5 Pillar programme: **The Feminine Energy Guide.**

The Pillars are titled:

🖤 Energy & The Chakras
🖤 Mindset Mastery
🖤 The Law of Attraction
🖤 The Magic of the Moon
🖤 Soul Connection & Spirituality

Together I will take you on an inner journey, to peel back the layers and uncover the true you that you have been longing to connect with. To give you everything you need to create your own spiritual toolkit, so you can make decisions from a heart centred, soul guided space and make confident choices that allow you to remain true to you on every level.

Now more than EVER we feel out of balance on so many different levels.

During the pandemic our lives have been turned upside down. We were given the gift of time, something most of us have never had enough of before.

We went inwards and reflected, we looked at the things that we would never have had the time to look at before and realised that actually, there were a few things that no longer made us happy anymore.

Does this resonate?

I am going to show you how to take a closer look at how YOU are feeling in your body, and WHERE you're feeling out of balance and out of alignment. How to look inside and FEEL where your energy is drawing you in. Where you are being invited to discover your inner light for what may be the first time ever.

Our energy is SO important, when our Chakras are out of balance it can affect not only our lives but the lives of all our loved ones too. We have been living so closely with people recently it's only natural that our energies are going to be affected.

I have created this pillar in the programme to help you understand how your beautiful body responds to energy and how easily it can be rebalanced so that you feel amazing and completely connected.

In the first pillar of my programme, I will be talking to you about energy and guiding you through each of the seven Chakras in depth, explaining where they are, what they represent, how to notice if they are off balance by the feelings and sometimes physical symptoms our body shows us.

There will be journal prompts throughout each of the sections for you to complete. This is to encourage you to create a deeper connection to yourself.

I want you to remember through this whole book that you cannot get this wrong, this is ***your own*** unique journey.

You will feel so free when you allow yourself to look inside and begin to discover your own beautiful body, to notice your own thoughts and hear your own voice.

To find your own inner light.

After this section you will feel so much more balanced and in control, and will understand so much more about your mind, body connection.

Eeeeeeeek! I love this section so much. Turn the page and let's get started!

15

PILLAR 1 ENERGY & THE CHAKRAS

WHAT EVEN IS A CHAKRA?

I'm going to start this section with the Science bit and then take you on a beautiful inner journey of self-discovery. I also have a little exercise that I want you to do before we start. I have put together a relaxing body scan meditation for you to read through and below there is a picture for you to mark down which part (or parts) of the body you were most aware of during the exercise.

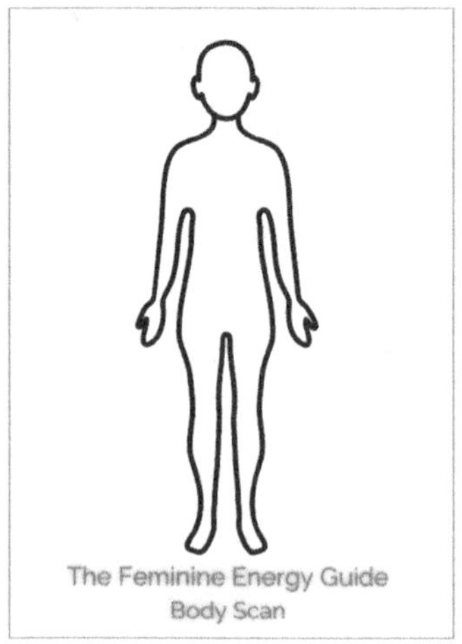

Are you ready?

Make sure you are somewhere comfortable where you won't be disturbed for a few minutes (If this is possible, if you have small people you may need to lock yourself in the loo, this is okay too).

Bring your awareness to your breath.

Now take a slow deep breath in through your n *everything* out through your mouth, relaxing your wh you exhale, and letting it feel really soft and heavy.

Give yourself permission to slow down, to take these next few minutes just for you, so you can really focus on how you are feeling. Make this your intention.

Take another slow breath in through your nose and as you exhale bring your awareness to the crown of your head. Relax your brow, relax your temples. Notice any areas of pressure or tension here too.

Relax your cheeks.

Relax your jaw.

Take a big slow breath in again and as you exhale bring your awareness to your neck.

The back of the neck.

The sides of the neck.

The front of the neck. Notice if there are any areas of tension here, how it feels to swallow.

Does it feel relaxed or is there any tightness?

Relax your shoulders. Relax the top of your arms, your elbows, your forearms, your wrists, the palms of your hands and all the way down to the tips of your fingers.

Now take another long, slow, deep breath in until you can't breathe in anymore and you feel like your lungs are filled with air, then as you exhale bring to attention into your heart space.

How does your heart feel? Is there any heaviness or sadness? Does it feel warm and fuzzy like it is full of love and happiness.

Take a minute to notice this now.

When you are ready breathe is slowly again this time softening your belly and allowing it to rise up, and hold it for a secon. Now slowwwwwwwly release the breath. As you do scan from the space just under your heart, your solar plexus, all the way down to the bottom of your belly.

Take your time.

How does this feel?

Is there any feelings of anxiety or emotion here? If there is can you take a moment to think about *what* exactly these emotions are and *where* have they come from?

Once you have done this continue to breath slowly and naturally as you bring your awareness to your hips. Deep inside to the very tip of your spine, your sit bones.

How does this feel for you here?

Do you have any sensations here?

Relax your legs, relax your knees, relax your ankles and your feet.

Then, when you are ready begin to take some bigger, deeper, fuller breaths, bringing some awareness back into your body now. You may want to have a big stretch and a yawn and have a little wriggle around to bring some energy back into the body.

When you are ready, make a note on the picture above of any places you had any sensations during that body scan.

You will be able to reflect back on this now throughout the next few chapters and use it as a guide as to what messages your body has been trying to tell you and see if they resonate.

Discovering the chakras and becoming more self-aware helped me to notice the subtle messages my body had been trying to give me for what was probably forever, to tell me that things weren't quite right on an energetic level.

The Chakras are energy centres in our bodies. They are little (and sometimes very big) spinning vortexes of energy that each have their own frequency.

The chakra system acts like a filter for our body. When they are out of sync with each other we can suffer in our energetic body, making us feel emotional, angry, and shitty. Each of the chakras relate not only to physical issues but to emotional issues too.

If one or more of the chakras gets blocked, your energy won't be able to flow freely through this system and this is where physical problems can develop.

All the negative vibes and shit that we come into contact within our daily lives affects us on so many different levels. Eventually, if we don't filter these out our little chakras start to become affected too. They get blocked and slow down which means that the flow of energy in our bodies becomes disrupted; creating knock-on effect with the other chakras.

Think of a garden hose, the water comes out the tap at one end, along the hose and out the other end. However, if the hose gets a block or a kink in it somewhere, it stops the water flowing and causes a big problem for the hose.

This is like the chakras. For example, if the throat chakra becomes blocked we can't speak our truth or say what we really want to. If we suddenly get a message from the heart chakra that needs to be spoken and there is a blockage, this message will never be received because it can't come out.

In a nutshell, the chakras are conductors of energy. Healthy chakras allow energy to flow freely through our physical body and our energetic system. The flow of this beautiful life force energy can easily be affected by our negative thoughts too.

Each chakra has encoded within it the pattern of our own attitudes and beliefs, which often blocks the life force energy, or stop it from flowing freely. It is our thoughts and attitudes more than anything else which block or release the flow of energy through the chakras.

Think for a moment of a time that you felt so happy and so in love that you could literally explode and there would be sparkly butterflies, glitter and shiny hearts EVERYWHERE!

Notice how this feels in your body. I bet you feel a bit warm and fuzzy, and I bet the corners of your mouth have turned up a little bit? You may have even, without realising, put one of your hands on your heart?

This is a positive thought, something that makes all the teeny tiny cells in your body smile and say, "Ahhhh". We like these.

Now think of a time when someone said or did something really mean to you. Notice how THIS feels in your body? I bet you can feel it sucking all the happiness out of your body. Making you feel like you're not good enough, waking up that inner bitch who is now laughing at you and scrambling around finding more evidence of times when you weren't good enough.

These are negative thoughts. Too many of these spikey buggers will easily make you feel like shit and block chakras.

Can you see the difference?

When we feel stuck in our lives, whether it's from insecurity, confidence issues, anxiety, fear or lack of spiritual awareness, it can be easy to accept this as the norm, because we have always felt this way. Sometimes even when we are aware of the chakras, we can tend to focus on the physical aspects that they affect, and not pay attention to the deep emotions that they are also connected to.

This is often because it hurts like a MOFO to look at the emotional stuff, so we continue to brush it under the carpet, take pain killers or whatever and crack on. I saw an image once of a man with a lion sat next to him chewing off his hand and it said, "Wow, those painkillers sure did take care of all the pain I was feeling. Now I can go back to work." Underneath it said in capitals, "TACKLE YOUR PROBLEMS, NOT JUST YOUR SYMPTOMS."

Unfortunately, you have to feel it to heal it. Sounds super cheesy but it's true.

Your body is SOOOOOOO clever. It will keep bringing up the same problem for you to look at again, and again, and again. Until you FINALLY can't ignore it anymore.

Like throwing a tennis ball into the bottom of the pool. It will sink at first, then gradually make it's way to the top of the water, building speed as it goes and then bob up through the surface with a big POP, and maybe a splash too.

That is what happens when we try and supress things. Our body is like, *I do NOT want to keep that in here thank you, so have it back AGAIN and AGAIN.... With even BIGGER symptoms and feely feels this time...sort it out FFS!*

Each of the chakras also relate to different emotions in the body, so depending on what emotion we are feeling, like jealousy or anger or sadness, will depend on which chakra it has an effect on. Or if like I just explained, you try and ignore it, it gets lodged in there and starts to become a block making you start to feel shitty.

So, without further ado, I introduce you to the Muladhura, the first of the chakras.

Mula =Root Adhara = Support

This little beauty is located at the base of the spine. (It is actually between your bum and your front bum, there are lots of different words that make me feel funny for this area so I will let you choose your own).

It is the colour red and is represented by the element of the earth. The root chakra connects us to our sense of being grounded, as well as our instincts of survival. Think of where it is too, it roots us to the earth when we sit down.

The Muladhara is the ROOT of the entire chakra system. It is the foundation on which all the others rest. If we don't balance the root chakra before we do the others, then any changes or development in our bodies will be without roots, ungrounded and will lack the stability that we require for true growth.

The root chakra relates to the earth element, and therefore all solid earthy things. For example, our bodies, our health, our survival, our material and monetary existence as well as our ability to manifest the things we want.

The root chakra's consciousness is all around survival. This means that this chakra acts as the maintenance programme of our bodies, protecting our health and our day-to-day mundane needs. Its focus is on the survival instinct so things like fear, hunger, the need for rest, shelter, and warmth. All the stuff we need to stay alive.

In today's life our survival instinct is not related anymore to lying awake at night to keep a fire alive, guarding our food from hungry beasts, or the fear of being dragged on into the darkness as some big creature's midnight snack.

Our environment may have changed but our survival instinct remains intact, but it's just a bit different now. Our survival instinct now is more about losing our job or not getting sick. All the situations we worry about nowadays can trigger our survival instinct and force our first chakra into panicking and working in overdrive.

When our survival is threatened the main emotion we experience is fear. Fear is the absolute demon of the first chakra. It completely counteracts the sense of safety and security that the root chakra brings. When this happens, we experience fear and other panicky emotions and the body reacts in a very negative way. This makes the root chakra become unbalanced.

When this happens and we bury our fears, or don't deal with how we are feeling this can fester and manifest itself into:

- Anger
- Irritation

- Restlessness
- Anxiety
- Depression
- Lack of focus
- Depression
- Money worries

Any fear trapped in the root chakra can eventually manifest into all these things. It can make you feel like you can't be yourself and can often make your feel like you are trapped and stuck in a rut.

The physical symptoms of a blocked root chakra are:

- Lower back pain. (My sciatic used to kick off when I was worried about money.)
- Eating disorders. (I would restrict myself because I was so out of control, this made me feel I had a bit of control left)
- Constipation.
- High Blood pressure.
- Bladder or kidney infections.

It is so important to recognise your fears and emotions and accept them and let them go. I know this sounds easier said than done, and it often is, because I have done it, and it's fucking solid sometimes.

And that's even more reason why you need to do it. You don't want that shitty energy lingering around in your body do you?

The root chakra starts to develop very early into childhood. If we have a traumatic childhood and are witness to or involved in any kind of verbal, mental or physical abuse this can get stuck in our little bodies and become trapped within this chakra.

So how do we heal the root chakra I can hear you asking?

We have to let go of our fears. Fears are generated by our thoughts most of the time. For example, how often have you lay in bed awake at night catastrophising and creating every scary scenario and tragic outcome possible? And the thing hasn't even happened!

Fear is also based on past experiences and our social conditioning, so if we have ever had a bad experience in the past, our clever memory stores it to remind us NOT to do the same thing again!

Social conditioning is all the things we have been told from our parents or elders as a child and just believed them without questioning. Like believing in Santa Claus or God. This might sound like a bonkers example, but my little girl has always been petrified of Santa Claus. She used to freak out at the thought of a man coming into her bedroom at night while she was asleep. (Perfectly normal and rational fear if you ask me.)

So, every year Santa never goes upstairs in our house and leaves her presents in the living room. We didn't tell her this to scare her obviously, but this is a tradition that we have been told for centuries isn't it, so we just continued it with our children, and she did NOT like it. We almost told her the truth, but I'm not going to say it out loud in case little eyes end up on this page.

Anyway, as I was saying, only when we learn to face our fears can we truly overcome them. (Unless your little and scared of

Santa.). This won't be pleasant, but you have to feel it to heal it.

Affirmations

Here are a small selection of positive affirmations that you can choose from to help you rebalance your root chakra.

I am not my thoughts.

I am always safe and secure.

I release my doubts and fears.

I am grounded.

I am healthy.

I am exactly where I am supposed to be.

Crystals

These little sparkly beauties make me squeak and pee glitter all over the place. I could honestly stare at them all day, and sometimes wish I had more arms so I could get more crystal bracelets on at the same time. I think the reason that bras and pockets were invented is so we can carry our crystals easily without anyone seeing and calling us weirdos.

Because crystals are formed in the earth, they have amazingly powerful healing properties. Each crystal has its own frequency and we are often drawn to certain crystals because we need some of what they have to offer. Some crystals can help us with grounding and are perfect to help us balance the root chakra. There are tons of these little beauties out there for you to discover to help with all of the other chakras too.

Crystals to help balance the Root Chakra are:

- Red Jasper: A nurturing stone that helps with mental strength, helps build resilience and gives you strength to handle stressful situations.
- Black Tourmaline: One of the most effective grounding and protective stones. It can help promote balance and stability and protects you against negative energies. It is also a fab little stress buster and helps eliminate tension in the body.
- Black Obsidian: A stone of strength and protection. It removes and purifies negative energies that have become lodged in your aura while also creating a shield preventing negativity from entering. It offers protection from both self-inflicted and environmentally induced negativity. And this clever little shiny can also help us to eliminate feelings of jealousy and anger.

Oooosh! So, there you have it, the foundation of your beautiful Chakra system.

Did any of it resonate?

Journal Prompt

I would love for you to do the guided meditation I shared with you are the start of this chapter for the next 21 days and keep a journal of how your beautiful body is feeling each day paying attention to which of the chakras are speaking to you.

Now you have a basic understanding of how you can notice, heal and rebalance your root chakra.

Are you ready to hear about my absolute FAVE Chakra the Sacral, let's dive in.

16

THE PORTAL OF LIFE

The second chakra in your gorgeous energy system is the Sacral Chakra. It is located in your lower belly right where your womb space is. The word sacral translates to "Sweetness" (I love this) and it develops between the ages of seven to fourteen years old. This space is all about connection and belonging. It represents emotions and feelings, boundaries, sexuality, intimacy, creativity, and self-acceptance.

The sacral chakra is a water element, it's all about letting go, going with the flow and letting our creative juices flow. It is the pleasure centre of the body, so if we are experiencing a LACK of pleasure in your day-to-day life and nothing seems to make you feel happy anymore, this can be a sign that your Sacral chakra needs some TLC.

This may be a touchy subject for some people, but as women sometimes we deny ourselves the things that will bring us pleasure. Like sex. Some women believe that embracing their sexuality is dirty or wrong, again this goes back to what they have been told or experienced growing up. But when you can truly embrace your feminine energy and surrender to these natural and sometimes intense desires, you light the fire within you, and you REALLY come alive.

Many of us do not take ANY time out for ourselves to do the things that we enjoy because we put other people's needs before our own. This is where boundaries come in. I will talk about boundaries in lots more detail later on in the book, but for the purpose of this section, when we put the importance of other people's happiness before our own it doesn't make our sacral chakra happy. AT all.

Symptoms of a blocked sacral chakra:

You may begin to feel stuck in a certain feeling or mood, like you just can't shift it and feel blocked like you can't move forwards. It's like that feeling of being in a funk! Like you are pissed off with everything and everyone and nothing you seem to do can shift it. (Think PMT)

Another sign that you're a little out of sorts in this area is when you become dependent on something that gives you pleasure. Often this is pleasurable things that aren't that good for you and this is the place where addictions are born. This could be addictions to people, substances, or bad habits and often these additions are created to block out emotions so that we don't feel what is going on. It could be an inability to feel our emotions, or that they are just TOO powerful and we want to shut them off.

We silence our mind with drink or drugs so that we can numb out the harsh reality of what we are experiencing. It proper sucks balls when you look at it like this.

It makes me sad that we are that so scared of FEELING, that we would rather choose something that is so bad for us that it detaches us from our senses. When addictions are present, we need to ask the question, "What need am I trying to fulfil? And is there a healthier way?" It may not be an easier way at first, as the change is a hard thing to do at the best of times, never mind when your head is hiding half-way up your arse, but there will almost always be a way that is better for your health.

This was me masking my emotions with drink and self-medicating. (Now I know why I couldn't get pregnant; I was totally shut down in this area.)

Another sign can be you are overly critical of yourself and sometimes give away your personal power to others to keep them close. This is often because you are craving connection and that feeling of belonging so much you are willing to give the person everything, they want to keep them. As women, it is often our sacral area that most men crave, if you get my meaning here. I am referring to our "sweet spot" which once given and not received with love, can often lead to much emotional pain afterwards.

Being taken advantage of hurts like a MOFO.

Memories of repressed emotions are held here too. These are all of the things that have happened to you throughout your life that you have either not been in a safe enough space to process or heal. Or have not wanted to look at, so have just pushed them down in the hope that they would stay buried deep in the depths of your mind (and body) forever and ever Amen!

Often once we start to look into our shadows, the place where we never dare to look, the darker side of us that we hide from others, we discover just how many emotions we have here. Most of the time they are put into a box inside our head, with a padlock on, and a big rock on the top to make sure they can never escape.

It can feel scary, but (here I go with the cheese again) you have to feel it to heal it.

When this sacred space is balanced you can experience deep pleasure in your life. You feel completely connected to the world around you and to your emotions.

You flow and expand.

You have healthy emotionally stable and safe relationships with others, and you are able to use your creativity in all areas of your life, bringing your dreams and visions into reality.

The sacral chakra is where we also hold our mother wounds. What is one of those I hear you ask? I want you to take a moment and think about the relationship you had with your mother.

What did it look like? How did it make you feel? Do your thoughts drift to the good times here, or do they instantly remember the bad?

Our mothers were vitally important role models in our development as little humans, and they helped us to form the very foundation of our emotional and our mental growth. To this very day, our mothers continue to influence us both through our deeply ingrained perceptions of life and through our feelings towards ourselves and other people.

And although our mothers may have tried their very best to show us love and to nurture us, our relationships with them may have felt like they were filled with more emotions like shame, guilt, and obligation. Like if we had to do things to please her to feel accepted.

In fact, we may still carry unresolved grief, fear, disappointment, and resentments towards our mothers long into our adult lives and this deep pain is usually the result of past generations of unhealed core wounds.

Our mother wounds are traumas that pass down from generation to generation that have a huge impact on our lives. When these are not healed, we pass the wounds that our mothers and grandmothers carried before us, unintentionally down to our own little people. These consist of toxic and regimental beliefs, ideals and perceptions. Finally, our children repeat the harming cycle, harming their own children.

This is why the sacral chakra is so crucial to our emotional wellbeing.

If your mother was emotionally unavailable for you, if she used to guilt to control you, was abusive in any way or made you feel like you were never good enough, this can cause a mother wound.

You may find yourself:

- Constantly comparing yourself and competing with other women.
- Self-Sabotaging when you experience happiness or success.
- Waiting for your mother's permission on an unconscious level to truly live your life the way you want to.
- The inability to speak your authentic truth and difficulty expressing yourself emotionally.

Because the Sacral chakra develops when we are very young (between the ages of seven to fourteen) mother wounds develop very early on in our lives. We are often bound by the belief that, "I was responsible for my mother's pain." and "I can make my mother happy if I am a good girl/boy.".

The truth is you are not and never were responsible for your mother's pain – only she is. Yet as children we are not aware of this and on a subconscious level many of us still feel guilty for being naughty, not good enough kids. These wounds are often deep and can sometimes take time to understand.

Ways to help heal the mother wounds are to:

- Let go of the idealistic visions and expectations you have of how a mother should be and realise that your mother is a human being trying to deal with her emotional pain as best she knows how.
- Remember that you can never change who your mother is, nor do you have the right to. That is 100% her responsibility. Stop waiting around for her to suddenly shower you with love, support, and validation if this has never happened before. You may feel like as you finally accept this is never going to happen that you experience grief of her absence and of all the things that you didn't have. Like the happy childhood you watched your friends have with their loving parents and the love you craved but didn't have.
- Find your own inner unconditional love for yourself. While you may not have received unconditional love from your mother, you can find it within yourself. When you truly love yourself, you can begin to shine a light on the limiting beliefs and perceptions you have

> about yourself and the world. Transforming your need for outer support to a deep inner acceptance. I am going to help you with this throughout the book.

Rebalancing your sacral chakra is SOOOOO much fun. It's all about honouring your creativity. We are naturally creative beings, so it's time to find out what really gets your juices flowing. It could be ANYTHING! Writing, drawing, colouring, experimenting with cooking, decorating, singing, or crocheting. ANYTHING that makes YOU smile.

Find your thing and give yourself time to do it. You totally deserve this.

Dancing is especially good for rebalancing the sacral chakra. Especially anything that involves shaking your hips. So get some Shakira on and have a shimmy round the house if you can. Think burlesque, maybe even a bit of twerking. Allow yourself to get a bit sexy.

Our womb spaces are created for holding and carrying our babies for nine months. This is also where we carry the residue of any unhealthy relationship energy. Many of us carry the trauma and shame of sexual abuse here too.

We have to give ourselves permission to heal. This divine feminine container is also where we hold grief, anger, shame and fear. When my mum passed away my period went really strange for months afterwards like I was actually grieving from my womb.

A beautiful way of healing this sacred space is by using visualisation. If you put your index fingers together and your thumbs together so they make a V shape, like what you would see if you imaged the shape of your womb, relax your other fingers around this shape and place your hands over your gorgeous belly.

Feel the warmth of your hands and visualise love and healing being sent from your hands into your womb space. You can even close your eyes and visualise the colour orange or an orange orb in your womb space receiving all this from your hands.

Journal Prompt

There are also some questions that you can ask yourself that will help you dig a little bit deeper into your healing:

- What sacrifices do you make to please others?

These dysfunctional relationships are toxic to both parties. You are always allowed to say No and you do not have to explain yourself to people. My mum used to say this to me all the time, and I never really got it until a few years ago. I think sometimes we put off saying no to people and say yes instead because we don't know what to say to them, and fear telling them the truth in case we upset them. The people pleaser in us shits herself and starts flapping, so it often feels easier to just say yes. I will talk more about this later in the book.

- Do you respect your female and male energy?

By this I mean it's perfectly OK to be soft one day and assertive the next. Different situations always require different responses too. Like sometimes we try and be calm with our kids and are in a nice fluffy kind mood, and then they continue acting like little nobends so you have to eventually go into full on sergeant major mode for them to even listen to what you are saying. We must do what we need to do when we need to do it.

- Are you a giver but refuse to receive gifts from others?

If this is you, I want you to think about this for a moment? How excited do you get when you are giving someone a gift? Sometimes I get so excited that when I see the person who I am giving the gift to I don't even say hello I just go up to them and shove the gift towards them with a big stupid grin on my face. A bit like a five-year-old who has made a car out of a margarine tub at school and is showing it to their mum.

- Something quite uncomfortable for some people, but sexual creativity is part of this chakra.

Do you talk to your partner enough about what makes you happy in the bedroom? Or what you would like to try? Get creative and have FUN.

Crystals to help balance the Sacral Chakra are:

- Carnelian: this helps you to have create focus and feel more powerful in situations where you feel unsure. Carnelian is also associated with fertility and can help to stimulate sexuality.
- Tigers Eye: Associated with courage and decisiveness, it helps you feel ready for any situation. So hopefully will poke your inner people pleaser in the eye.
- Orange Calcite: Highly associated with creativity, it has a warming, nurturing effect and can help remove

blocks and gain more clarity when dealing with difficult decisions.
- Moonstone: One of my faves and my birth stone as I am a Cancerian, this stunning moonstone has such a beautiful feminine energy. It helps to get your creative juices flowing and increases intuition.

You can place these crystals on your sacral chakra (not all at the same time though, pick one you are drawn too and use that one), close your eyes and focus your attention on this area, envisioning it unblocking and energy flowing freely. It feels like magic.

We are now moving up to the last of the chakras that represent the physical body, our little powerhouse the Solar plexus Chakra.

17

THIS LITTLE LIGHT OF MINE

Just before we delve into this little beauty, I want to explain something about these bottom three chakras.

The bottom three are connected to the earth, the water, and the fire within us. They keep us grounded and allow us to feel a physical connection to the world. They are our foundations and our base that keeps us physically, emotionally, and mentally balanced and aligned.

The solar plexus chakra is the third chakra in our bodies, and the final physical chakra that connects us physically to our bodies.

From the heart up we go into the spiritual chakras that connect us to source/the divine/God -whichever of these feels right for you.

The Manipura - as it is called in Sanskrit - translates to "lustrous gem". It is associated with our personal power and is where our Ego is born. From the ages of fourteen to twenty-one this little sparkly chakra begins to discover its potential and decides if it will become loud and lairy and a know-it-all (like most teenagers) or a little wall flower who doesn't like to be seen.

I had so much anxiety as a teenager, I had no self-esteem and was unbelievably self-conscious. If I could go back to my teenage-self now and tell her how bloody beautiful she was inside and out I would do it in a heartbeat. I constantly compared myself to everyone else and had zero self-confidence - unless I had had a drink - then I was the life and soul of the party, up for anything, especially a dare, which got me into a bit of hot water on several occasions.

The solar plexus also represents our personal power and our identity. It's where we carry our feelings of independence and self-assurance and is the main contributor in how we make decisions. It is our centre of personal empowerment.

Signs that your little gem is blocked are:

- When you don't know what you want.
- When you need input from people and their opinions before you move forward and make up your mind about something.

Think of a time when you have had to make a really difficult decision. Think of the feelings that came up for you at that time. You may have felt indecisive and worried about what other people will think of your decision, scared of making a mistake or getting it wrong and people judging you for being a failure. You may have talked yourself out of doing it at all because you have no self-belief or self-confidence.

Fear shows up massively in this chakra, and it can hold us back for our whole lives if we don't see it for what it is.

- Fear of judgement
- Fear of failure
- Fear of change
- Fear of rejection.

This is something that stopped me for so long. When I first started my Facebook group and I wanted to go live, I remember sitting in my little studio crying on the phone to my business coach. I was so petrified of what people would think of me and what they would say. Like "Who does she think she is?" and "Look at the state of her.". I didn't like my nose or my teeth, and I would cringe every time I heard my voice played back to me. I just wanted to hide in the cupboard.

It also triggered old wounds in me from being bullied. I worried about the bullies seeing me and coming back to make fun of me again. How bonkers is this! I was a grown woman still playing out all these childhood fears but until we really look at them we won't be able to heal them.

Healing really is a lifelong journey.

Just when we think we have cracked it and we feel a bit confident, some negative memory leaks out of a little crack and shouts, "TA DA!!" And back in the cupboard we go!

This chakra is one of the most commonly blocked chakras in all the clients I have seen over the years, simply because of the millions of overwhelming things that life throws at us.

Feelings of unworthiness and feeling powerless in your actual being is another sign. You may have been in victim mode and feel like you have always been pushed around by others, or made fun of for the choices you made, so you second guess yourself and now need the approval of other people in your life when making any personal choices or decisions.

You may have negative self-talk and even feeling of anger and resentment.

Sometimes we can give away our personal power if we want someone to like us. The people pleaser in us steps forwards with their bestest shoes on and offers themselves out fully to the approval and acceptance of whoever they are trying to make like them or to please.

This is almost always at the cost of part of your heart or your soul. Or both.

Narcissism is born here too. The other side of the coin to this passive, indecisive, unconfident little wall flower is the arrogant, overbearing, abrasively in your face cock-sure ego maniac and if this behaviour continues welcome the narcissist.

The person who seeks power over others, who is always right and will not think twice about making an absolute twat of you in a room full of people if it means that they would look better than you. The chatter of shit and lover of their own voices. The spikey energy you feel entering a room without even having to look to see who it is.... You can just FEEEEEL them. The cold tingly sensation creeping up your back and over your shoulders like a thousand crawly spiders, then the spike of anxiety that consumes your whole body and you realise they are now here.

Physical symptoms of the solar plexus being out of sync are:

- Overeating and general overindulgence.
- Laziness.
- A need to control everything and everyone.
- Intolerance and competitiveness.
- Lack of focus.
- Digestive problems like ulcers or indigestion.
- Low body weight and low energy.

When the Solar plexus chakra is balanced, we feel confident, decisive and we have very good boundaries for ourselves and for other people. We realise that we do not need to use or abuse our power to be in control on other people or situations, and we also recognise this to be true for ourselves.

We don't allow people to take advantage of us and we politely and kindly find it incredibly easy to say NO! Without feeling guilty or plunging ourselves into an instant feeling of fear in case we have hurt the other persons feelings.

Mrs People Pleaser has been tied and gagged, shoes removed and gently placed with love into the cupboard. You are also able to put plans into action towards your dreams because you can make decisions and are no longer dithering around. You KNOW what you want and what is right for YOU and you are READY! YES GIRL!

You feel motivated and have purpose and a feeling of peace with life like you are exactly where you should be and you are so frickin' full of self-love and self-empowerment. You can express yourself with personality, really owning your truth and feeling it with every iddy biddy cell in your beautiful body.

You have clarity and you are 100% authentically YOU.

And it feels fucking amazing.

When you realise that you do *not* have to please anyone but yourself, and I don't mean being a knob and being selfish or mean, I mean that you have realised that this is YOUR life, and that only YOU are the one who can make these changes that are going to make YOU happy and by GOD you are ready to get this fucking show on the road!! Yeeeeeeehah!!

How to balance Chakra Number 3:

- **Affirmations**

Affirmations are such powerful little gifts that we can give to ourselves, and they work best when you are looking in the mirror at yourself, right into your own eyeballs. At first this will probably feel cringy and reeeeeeally uncomfortable, but if you can allow yourself to have this connection it is honestly unbelievable.

They say the eyes are the window to the soul, so when we look at ourselves into our own eyes, we are looking right into our own souls. The first time I looked into my own eyes and said out loud the words, "I am enough!" I burst into tears. It came from nowhere and was a big uncontrollable sob that lasted for a good few minutes. Well, it probably did come from somewhere. It had probably been waiting inside to hear those words my whole life, and when I said them it was like, "FINALLY!!"

The words I AM are unbelievably powerful. It speaks of things in the present tense and when used in affirmations or as part of the Law of Attraction (which we will be covering in detail later on in the book) it draws in positive energy and can help you to attract the things that you desire or the person you long to be.

Here are some affirmations:

I believe in myself.

I am enough.

I can accomplish anything I desire.

I am worthy of love and affection.

I am a good person.

I am strong.

I am confident.

I am empowering myself more every day by making positive choices.

I am the creator of my dreams.

And you can easily add your own bit that feels right for you and resonates with what is going on in your world right now after the I AM... make it personal to you and you can change these every day depending on how you are feeling.

Crystals for the Solar Plexus chakra are:

- Citrine: Associated with positivity and optimism, which is not surprising given its cheerful yellow colour. It's often used to assist in manifesting abundance, especially money and positive opportunities. It awakens the solar plexus chakra, helping to create confidence helping the person embrace and stand in their own personal power.

- Tigers eye: Helps to release fear and anxiety and aids harmony and balance. It stimulates taking action and helps you to make decisions with discernment and understanding, and unclouded by your emotions.
- Yellow calcite: Associated with self-confidence and hope. It is said to be effective at clearing out old energy patterns and increasing personal motivation and drive. Yellow Calcite is also a stone that will connect you to your own spirit guides.

This solar plexus chakra was a biggy for me when I started my healing journey, and still is. I am constantly aware of my inner bitch being present and that I am chatting complete hairy testicles to myself. I am SOOO grateful that I am self-aware enough to see this when it is happening now, because for years I spoke so unkindly to myself.

Self-sabotage and comparisionisitis are massive indicators that you need some serious TLC in your life and remember that once we have healed, rebalanced and aligned these chakras it not all done and finished. Our lives are so turbulent that we will *always* need constant maintenance, but when we can SEE it as it is happening we don't end up in the cupboard with a bottle of vodka. We can tell our inner bitch to, "Fuck off!" because we know the things that we are telling ourselves are not true and are often based on fear.

Anyway, I will take you a little higher now into the spiritual centre of your entire chakra system. The Heart.

18

INNER BITCH

Let's talk about that inner bitch for a minute before we move into the heart chakra. She needs to be seen for what she is.

And I could not be writing this at a more perfect time.

As I sit here typing these words my own inner bitch is standing behind me reading over my shoulder and reminding me how shit I am, and who the fuck do I think I am, and that nobody is going to buy my book so I may as well not bother.

She is an absolute nob end.

She shows up every time I get a bit excited about doing something that is making me want to proper pee glitter everywhere. She steps in front of me with a smarmy face and smirks at me, looking at me like I am something crusty she has just picked from underneath a school desk. (I bet you pulled a face then too?)

Also known as inner critic, mind monkeys, superego, shit chatter, boring Brenda, cunty Karen. It's whatever you want to call them, her, him. (Sorry to anyone called Brenda or Karen, no offence intended at all!)

They pop up every time we allow our insecurities and imperfections to get the better of us, and with sheer delight and excitement proceed to piss all over our dreams and fizzle out any excitement we may have had. She makes you feel so insecure that you just want to hide up your own hole and not bother doing anything at all. Mine shouts me down, judges me, makes me doubt myself and sometimes actually makes me shout, "Fuck off!" out loud!

But the difference is that I see her now for what she is. Even though she speaks in my voice to me, I know that her words are not mine. She is there trying to stop me from doing things I have never done before because she is scared. I used to listen to her and let her words affect me, I had no self-confidence, I would constantly shame myself about how shit I was at everything, and I believed everything she said.

But now when she turns up it means that something is triggering me somewhere. So I take myself off and meditate for ten minutes and see if I can reveal what is going on? Sometimes I do find out, sometimes I don't. But I always show myself a lot more love and kindness than I normally would when she turns up.

Just be aware of what you are saying to yourself. Your thoughts are incredibly powerful and have a huge impact on what happens in your body. Like with the cells, feeling happy when we think happy thoughts and feeling sad when we think sad thoughts.

You are in control of this too.

You just need to remember that you are.

And choose not to listen to your inner bitch chatting shit to you.

19

THE BRIDGE BETWEEN TWO WORLDS

Your heart chakra is the central balance point of your whole chakra system and is the heart of your very being. Your heart chakra is what keeps you in perfect balance between spirit and physical matter.

Where the Divine meets the material.

It is the portal through which you can connect to the light of your soul and the love and guidance from the angelic realm. It is the spiritual system of your entire chakra system. It is your internal compass that guides you through life, helping you to stay in perfect sync and on your highest path of love where you feel open to believing anything is possible. When we can come from this place of love, we cannot get it wrong. Love is what makes the world and our lives such a beautiful place.

The beautiful function of this chakra is to balance the upper and the lower chakras so that you feel aligned, in perfect balance, and live your life in harmony. When it is functioning properly you feel positive, you are vibrating at a higher frequency and gratitude oozes through your veins.

You have compassion.

You have kindness.

You believe that life has a purpose.

Your heart is your energy centre for unconditional love, your inner portal to the realms of peace and divine connection .

It is what allows you to give and receive love, and this is why keeping your heart open is such an important practice. So that you can truly and deeply connect to others and live a balanced, happy and fulfilled life.

It is your heart that helps you to stay balanced, allowing you to walk your spiritual path while never losing sight of the importance of staying grounded and connected to the physical world. Like I said the bridge between the physical and the spiritual.

What does it do?

The heart chakra connects you to source/the universe/God, whatever you want to call it and reminds you that through being present and having a *Higher* awareness that you are *One* with all. That is your deepest and highest truth. As the spiritual centre of the chakra system the heart chakras main themes are:

- Healing
- Compassion
- Relationships
- Love

This heart chakra healing is connected on all levels (emotional, physical, mental, spiritual.) It allows you to love freely and openly and most importantly to process your emotions properly. It opens you up to your spiritual gifts and it's role is to connect you to your unique soul qualities, soul gifts and abilities.

When your heart chakra is balanced you are grounded in your truth and operating from your highest divine self. This healing allows you to live from an open heart. Think of that warm fuzzy feeling you get when you feel love towards someone. It feels so light and right, like you KNOW it to be true.

You become more rooted in compassion, you can feel your heart smile as this love is reflected back to you, mirroring and remembering that we are all connected and we are all one.

The Hindu saying "Namaste" means the light in me honours the light in you. Or I like to say in my yoga classes, "The light in my heart honours that light in your heart, as we are one!"

Balancing your heart chakra aligns you to your passion, purpose and the endless possibilities that have always been available to you in the divine timeline. When you are connected to the core of your heart, it allows you to move and flow through life feeling all hippy dippy with love and lightness in your being. Yeh man!

And love feels so fucking good doesn't it?

Just sit for a minute and close your eyes, take a few deeps breaths to ground into yourself and then think of someone you really love? Or a happy memory of love, or a thing that you love.

How does it feel?

I bet some of you have subconsciously put your hand onto your hearts without even realising.

Love to me feels warm and glowy from the inside out, it makes me feel like I could sparkle like Tinkerbell from Peter Pan.

Symptoms of a blocked heart chakra:

The most common symptom of a blocked heart chakra is feeling disconnected to your emotions. Like when something happens that *should* really make you feel all the feels, but you don't actually give two turds?

Sometimes when our heart has had its fair share of pain and being stomped on one too many times, it eventually thinks, "Fuck this shit!" and builds its own little fortress, enclosing itself inside what is known in the world of healing as a spiritual heart wall. Think of the olden times when there is a big cobble stone wall surrounding a castle, it has a moat around the outside full of hungry snappy crocodiles lurking below the surface, and there is no way in unless whoever is inside lowers the draw bridge.

Your heart is the one on the inside refusing to lower the draw bridge, in fear of being stomped on again. BUT what happens here is although nothing gets in, nothing gets out either.

Being in the fortress is very, very, lonely, so you eventually begin to miss the love that you once felt. But just as you are about to lower your draw bridge, traumatic memories flood your hearts little mind, and it remembers the pain.

So, it stays inside where it is safe. But it is unbelievably lonely. If nothing is being received, nothing can be given either so everyone looks at the person who has the heart inside the castle with the fortress around it and the moat with snappy crocodiles in and thinks, "They are one fucking HEARTLESS bitch!"

But the truth is, you have been hurt and this is a natural defence mechanism for the heart to do this.

Sometimes what also gets trapped inside is forgiveness. Your heart sees this as a weakness and feels that the other people don't deserve to be forgiven but forgiveness doesn't excuse their actions, forgiveness stops their action from destroying your heart.

There is a saying, "Forgive others, not because they deserve it, but because you deserve peace." Holding onto these negative emotions only hurts us. The other person has no idea we have all this resentment, and anger and pure *pissed offness* bubbling around inside of us. Instead, as we relive the thing they did or said that we can't let go of time and time again, our mind doesn't recognise that this isn't real, so as we feel our way through each part of the scenario of bodies release all the same stress hormones as if it were ACTUALLY happening.

Sweet Lord! Imagine what this is doing to our bodies!

Stress overload!

You may also have something that you yourself have done that you are struggling to forgive yourself for.

Remember that you are human.

Remember that you acted the best way that you could at that time, with the knowledge you had and made the decision you made and there is NOTHING that you can do to go back and change this now. Reliving it and shaming yourself and feeling guilty and embarrassed and in fear still of what other people will think of you is just NOT going to change anything or make it go away.

You have to forgive yourself.

Looking back now if you know that you would not have done those things, know that this is because you have now grown as a person. You are NOT the same person that you were back then when this happened. Twist it around. Be grateful for the better insight and awareness that you now have, and for the opportunity to make better choices from now on as you have grown as a person.

Accept that this happened.

Fully accept yourself in this situation looking at it with this new lens. It is OK that this happened. It was an experience that you needed to have to show you whatever it was you needed to see or learn. Allow yourself to be at peace with the whole situation.

Try putting your hand on your heart and saying either out loud or to yourself, "I forgive myself."

Forgive yourself for what you didn't know, or what the other person didn't know. So many of us live in a state of holding a grudge or resentment and self-blame.

Journal prompt

It hurts so much when we hold onto stuff. Tell your story, write it all down maybe and really untangle it out of your head and release it from your heart. Then don't read it back. Fold the paper over, get a little candle (SAFETY FIRST PLEASE PEEPS) and allow the flame to ignite and devour it. Let it go!

Or if you have typed it out, again don't read it back as this allows all of the emotions and energy you have released while writing it to be absorbed back into your body, highlight the whole file and press DELETE!

GONE!

SEE YA MOTHER FUCKER!

And now breathe. And feel into the realisation that YOU ARE NOT YOUR PAST!

Another way to help heal and rebalance your heart chakra is to show yourself the love and compassion that you would show to other people. Treat yourself exactly the same, and give yourself the same kind, loving, nurturing advice that you would give your bestest friend.

This is something that I do now, especially as I am now my own boss.

If I wake up and am feeling all the feels and know that my cup only has a little spitty dreg at the bottom and I need that for myself to get through the rest of the day, then I clear my diary. My energy is so important to me now. And if I don't have anything for myself, how am I going to have anything for anyone else?

It really is that simple. Go with how you feel.

If someone came to you and said, "I'm feeling a bit ropey today, I feel a bit anxious and emosh but not sure why, and "m sooooo tired?" I would say to them "Come here and give us a hug. Now go and get into bed and have a nap and when you wake up if you will feel the same, we can have more hugs, a cuppa and talk about it."

But often if this is US feeling this way, we just plough on. Using the bare fumes that we have inside of us, hoping that our mask doesn't fall off if someone notices or says something nice to us and we cry all over them!

Self-love is the ultimate self-care.

Other signs of an unbalanced heart chakra are:

- Jealousy and judgement.
- Low self-esteem.
- Being critical or controlling.
- Being suspicious or feeling possessive.
- Being defensive and not being able to trust.
- Being afraid to let go of emotional hurt.

Journal Prompt

Look at all of these emotions and think how they can relate to past hurt or trauma of the heart that you may have experienced in your life. Make any notes about what comes up for you, try not to over think it and just write down what come up. Remember you cannot get this wrong.

Relationship issues

If you regularly experience draining or problematic relationships this can make it difficult for you to connect to people as you are constantly having your heart poked and prodded until it goes into a state of blocking EVERYTHING that is coming in to save you from any more pain.

Fear of intimacy is another sign things aren't as they should be. This is often again caused from past hurt. The way to overcome this is to be present; stop living in the past. Start loving yourself and look forwards instead of backwards. You're not going that way.

How to heal and rebalance the heart chakra:

- **Show yourself love.**

Showing yourself some love and practising self-care routines are an amazing way to help you heart to heal. There is no cookie cutter for this process, *you* do what works for *you*.

My self-care looks like many different things depending on what I need. Sometimes it will be clearing my diary and having a digital detox, and other days it will be a long bath with my book or a nap in the middle of the day.

Do what is best for you. Think about WHAT YOU need.

- **Be open with your emotions.**

If you feel like you want to kick the shit out of someone or are raging and need to scream, get a pillow go into a room on your own, shut the door and SCREEEEEEEEEEAM into your pillow until you get it alllll out.

Scream therapy is actually a thing and feels fucking amazing.

If you can't do it at home go out in the car, turn the music up loud and scream like a banchee. It kinda feels like you're being a bit of a rebel when you scream, because I don't know about you but screaming wasn't a thing that was really allowed in my house when I was a kid. So doing it now makes me feel free.

- **Be honest with yourself.**

The more emotions that you repress the more pain that is being trapped inside. And believe me it will feel totes amazeballs when you release all that heaviness you have been carrying around with you for God knows how many years.

It makes you feel like you can take a big, deep, expansive, beautiful, breath.

- **Acceptance**

Practising acceptance is another superpower that we can incorporate into our lives.

Accepting life as it is happening to you and having acceptance of yourself exactly where you are at is the most compassionate thing you can do.

It is such a powerful spiritual tool. Just give yourself permission for whatever it is you need to accept.

Don't fight it.

- **Work on letting go.**

When we can let go of some of the dark heavy painful stuff, it creates space for all the good stuff to come in.

Recently the shamanic healing work that I have done with some of my clients to help them release and shift old energy has been so transformational. They have had huge shifts in their lives and had unbelievable surges of fresh sparkly energy that they have been able to inject into their relationships or work.

- **Gratitude**

If you can get into the habit of expressing gratitude whenever you can in your life, this will make your heart sparkle and smile. Infecting all the people around you with your beautiful energy. More on gratitude later in the book.

- **Random acts of kindness**

This is one of my mostest favouritest things to do EVER!

I love doing unexpected kind things for other people that make their heart smile.

Like buying my friends presents, or even just sending them a message telling them how grateful I am to have them in my life. I have helped to pay towards someone's shopping when they didn't have enough money before too. It makes me feel so warm and fuzzy.

Crystals for the Heart chakra are:

Rose quartz: This in my absolute go to crystal when my heart is feeling heavy or sad. I have worn a rose quartz bracelet every day since my mum died and if I don't have it on, I can feel the difference. Rose quartz helps to heal your heart, helps with compassion and unconditional love.

Green Aventurine: Another bracelet that I wear every day. This is a fantastic protection crystal for healers. It helps to keep your emotional body calm in trying situations and provides strength confidence and courage.

Journal Prompt

We are at the halfway point now with the heart being the middle chakra, and I would love for you to take a minute to notice how much of what you have read so far has really hit home for you.

Which of the four chakras you have learned about so far has been the one that made you go

"OMG, that's totally ME!" What things can you take from this to start to make changes to bring your chakras into alignment?

20

SPEAK YOUR TRUTH WOMAN AND OWN THAT SHIT

I have struggled with speaking my truth pretty much my whole life. This goes hand in hand with being a people pleaser and not wanting to share what I really thought in case I upset or offended anyone. Even if they were saying nasty shit to me, the, "Always be polite and remember your manners like a good girl." saying had been drummed into me from a child and made me feel restricted and silenced.

This caused me MAJOR ISSUES in all my relationships as I always put everyone else before myself.

The Throat Chakra is our communication centre. Regarded as the bridge from the heart to the soul, the Sanskrit word for it is Vishuddha and translated it means, "to purify" as in being able to speak your truth with kindness and compassion. It identifies with the colour blue.

To speak our truth, we must first be grounded, emotionally stable, confident, and come from a place of love, this is why it is important to balance the chakras from the root upwards. Our voice allows us to speak or sing our love for our partner, our family, our faith, and the world. On the flip side, if we are not balanced in these areas, we may notice our words are not very kind, we may chat shit about people and speak mainly bitter and negative words.

Mastering the throat chakra helps us to understand just how important it is to speak kindly and how when we can become self-aware and notice how WE feel, we then have the confidence to share our emotional messages with other people, even if it's not what they want to hear, if keeping it in means we are going to endanger our throat chakra they need to be told!

When the throat chakra is balanced people recognise their right to express their hurt or anger but do it in a way that doesn't belittle or make the other person feel like shit. In a nice way basically. They can use both their heart and their mind at the same time when speaking to others. They understand the power of the spoken and the written word and take full responsibility for their actions and other people's feelings.

They speak from a place of compassion and know that if others don't *hear* what they have to say that it doesn't mean they haven't said their message correctly but that the other person is not ready or at a stage in their lives where they can take on board what is actually being said. They express themselves clearly and with purpose. They understand the powerful energy associated with negative words and comments so choose their words with intention.

There is a fantastic experiment done by the great Dr Masaru Emoto. He claims that human's speech and thoughts have dramatic effects on water, and that when water is exposed to positive happy language and thoughts and frozen it creates the most beautiful symmetrical visually pleasing ice crystals, and that negative intentions resulted in the opposite and created blurry, ugly crystals. This is really interesting because we as humans are made up of approximately 70% water, so the thoughts and feelings we have towards others REALLY do matter.

Here is the link to a you tube clip explaining his experiment: https://youtu.be/Moz82i89JQw

I would love to know what you think.

Signs of a blocked Throat Chakra:

Sometimes when the throat chakra is blocked people can have a lot of trouble speaking and expressing themselves in front of other people. They may hold their chin down towards their chest and speak quietly, hiding their throat chakra like a shy child. This shows that the person has a vulnerability in that area, so they are shielding it by keeping their head down as they speak.

Their words make them nervous because they will often fear the response they get from people. They feel scared to share their opinions, and if they try to join in group conversations they speak quietly with no enthusiasm and are often 'not heard'.

Blocked chakras can stem from being told as a child that *children should be seen and not heard*, or to *shut up* all the time by older siblings or dominant parents. Perhaps when you have spoken in the past you have been laughed at or shamed by older siblings or parents who made fun of you. To cope with the rejection of your *True Self* as a child you suppress it and keep suppressing it.

The sad child remains locked within you in adult form, and this can make you neglect responsibility for growing up and taking any sort of control in your life. Being too scared to make decisions so letting other people take the lead and often ending up doing things you didn't want to because you were too scared to say what you really wanted, in case it wasn't what they wanted to hear and you would offend them.

This can then stay with you like a trauma and continues into adult hood. The fear of speaking in front of people in case this happens is often HUGE. I know it was for me for a LONNNNNNNG time. I was repeatedly shamed by the school bully and then again by the Dictator in my adult life.

My poor throat chakra was in tatters.

Another sign of a blocked throat chakra is someone clearing their throat constantly, like they are being choked by the truths that they are having to swallow. On a physical level it can manifest in the body as sore throats, tonsilitis, tooth aches, a stiff neck and thyroid problems. Sometimes even overeating, we physically stuff food in our mouths to silence ourselves.

You may also find that you say, 'Yes' a lot when actually you mean, 'No'. You can feel it in your body can't you, the moment you say the words and every cell in your body screams "NOOOOOOO!! What are you doing?" and quickly curl up into a ball.

Sometimes you may find the word, "Yes" just coming out of your mouth before you have even realised what you are saying yes to, because you are that used to just agreeing with everything. Even if you have a million and one things to do already and are full to capacity, you STILL take on other people's requests because you don't want to disappoint them but end up stressing the shit out of yourself because you don't know how you're going to get it all done!

What happens here is that the frustration and the resentment and the anger then builds up here too. Because if we can't say no to someone were not going to be able to tell them how pissed off we are about them asking us to do stuff for them, when they can CLEARLY SEE we are already too busy!

Some people genuinely do just take the piss don't they?

Sometime people's throat chakras can be too open, giving out *too* much energy. We all have a friend who is a little bit gobby and gossipy don't we. The excessive talker, who constantly interrupts because they have too many thoughts and doesn't listen to anything anyone else is saying. They can even come across as a little bit arrogant and cocky as they are completely unaware of other people's feelings. They often speak inappropriately, tell lies, and spend too much time trying to make themselves heard. When your throat chakra is overactive you are your own *and* others worst critic and don't use your words with thought or consideration. Sometimes they can be like little arrows fired towards people and stabbing them right in the heart. As my mum used to say, "Some people speak before they engage their brains!"

Ways to balance the throat chakra:

Balancing this chakra can be really fun. One of my favourite ways is to sing.

If you imagine the throat chakra to be blocked, as we sing and vibrate our little vocal cords the vibration releases negative energy and rebalances the throat chakra. Sometimes rather than singing depending on how intense you are feeling shouting or screaming into a pillow can be done instead. This feels amazing if you have been feeling frustrated about something you have not been able to say, like if someone has really got on your tits but you haven't been able to tell them.... try this one.

Chanting is another way. I really love chanting, I did it for a few weeks when it was recommended to me by my Buddhist friend Carole, and it was amazing. Scientific studies have also found that chanting can decrease stress, anxiety, and symptoms of depression, as well as increasing positive mood, feeling of relaxation and focused attention. If you want to have a go, I recommend trying it when you are on your own, as I felt like a bit of a nutter when I first tried it but I noticed the results instantly.

You can chant anything too, a positive affirmation, like Om, or hop onto you tube and have a go of a Buddhist chant if that takes your fancy. I used to chant Nam Myoho Renge Kyo, it is associated with the awakened heart of the universe. I liked the way it felt as I said it, but you can find what is right for you.

Journaling is another amazing way to clear the throat chakras and is something that I do a lot. Every day in fact. Sometimes we have been unable to say the words we have wanted to speak for whatever reason, but by expressing these words in a written form we can allow their energetic frequency to leave our minds and our bodies by simply brain dumping it all out on paper.

You can even write a letter to a person who has done something to you in the past. The person that you have never been able to tell how they made you feel, or how they hurt you. Don't over think it, just get it all out.

And then if it is something particularly traumatic do NOT read it back.

Simply rip it up and burn it and as the smoke goes up into the air, imagine this is infused with all of the negative energy that has left your body, and you are now free of this. This is called Gifting and is very powerful for trauma release in people who simply cannot speak what has happened to them. But you mustn't read it back, or the energy of what you have just released can go back into your body.

This is something that worked really well for me. I found gifting so healing and releasing. And I didn't realise *how much* stuff I had been holding on to. I would sometimes cry as I was writing. (I do cry a lot as you have probably noticed, I am totally fine with this.)

Other ways are:

- Becoming aware of the language and words that you are using. Are they kind, true or necessary?
- Shoulder and neck rotations to open the throat and relax any tension in the neck
- Affirmations (see affirmations section at the back of the book.)
- Listening to someone fully for 5 minutes. REALLY listening, not interrupting, and paying full attention. Then swap over.
- Laughing – Watch some funny stuff. I love watching people slipping on ice in the winter, not so that they hurt themselves, just so that they slide backwards down the hill after it has taken them all day to get to the top. Makes me chuckle.

Crystals for the Throat chakra are:

- Lapis Lazuli: It is a powerful thought-provoking stone that helps you to reveal your inner truth. It is also a stone of serenity and strength.
- Larimar: A stunning pale swirly blue stone that represents the sea and the sky energy, but also the goddess energy. It is tranquil and relaxing and allows you to speak your truth with kindness.

The colour blue is associated with the throat chakra and there are honestly so many beautiful blue crystals you can choose from, have a look online and see which ones you are drawn too.

We are now entering the chakra that houses the seat of your soul, the third eye chakra. Where intuition and dreams come from.

21

THE SEAT OF YOUR SOUL

We are truly in the spiritual realms of self-connection now. SQUEEEEEE!

The Third eye chakra is situated in between your brow.

If you gently raise your eyes upwards, not too much so that you strain your eyeballs, there is like a little sweet spot. This is the seat of your soul, known as Anja in Sanskrit. Often called the brow chakra because of its location. It is represented by the beautiful colour of indigo, the energy of deep change, wisdom and inner knowing. It translates as 'To perceive or command' and is associated with consciousness.

It allows us to see something and make up our own mind about what we have seen. Creating our *own* reality. Consciousness is the state of being aware and responsive to *your* surroundings. It is your own unique thoughts, feelings, sensations, and awareness of *your* surroundings.

ONLY YOURS!

This means the third eye is capable of seeing AND creating. Bringing your dreams to life by seeing them with the third eye, speaking them with the throat, feeling them in your heart, having the confidence to create them with your solar plexus, birth them and bring them into the world with your sacral and root chakra.

Its vibration allows you to draw the energies of the lower chakras up into higher spiritual vibrations. It is the connection to the divine, to source, to God. It is associated with unconditional love by seeing the truth – that we are all one.

This aspect of consciousness is best known as clairvoyance. Clairvoyance is the act of clear seeing, the ability to see through the noise of material things in the world that create our limited sense of time and space. Moving all of the obstacles out of the way.

The lower four chakras represent the earth, water, fire and air, while the top three chakras, the throat, the brow and the crown are what is known as the spiritual or the Ether Chakras. Ether represents both space within and outwards too. The throat chakra is a gentle vibration, but the third eye is a higher and faster vibration, faster than sound which is associated with the throat.

The third eye vibrates at a frequency we perceive as visible light.

From all the energy of the elements we have seen so far (by elements I mean earth, wind, water, fire) light is by far the fastest of them all. It transcends our sense of time. Basically of all the chakras are spinney and the third eye is one of the spinniest.

When I meditate sometimes, I get a light but warm tingly sensation in my third eye, this means that it is activating and I sometimes lose sense of time as I float off into wherever I go as I float away with my thoughts.

What is revealed in the third eye chakra when it is balanced?

Intuition

Inner tuition, our inner teacher. I like to also call this my spidey senses. It guides us without us realising it is guiding us. Like I just KNOW something, without knowing how or why or even feeling that I need to question myself, I just KNOW!

Have you ever had this feeling before? I have been in some tricky situations in the past when I was a teenager, and if I had gone with my intuition when it was screaming at me to, "LEAVE NOW!" some of them would never have happened.

This is now what I share with my kids, even though they are twelve and eight I say to them, "If you ever feel unsafe or that you need to leave but you don't know why, don't' question it, just do it! Ring me wherever you are and whatever time it is and I will always come and get you. I will NEVER be angry with you for asking me to come and get you either.".

I wish I had been told that when I was a child.

Do you trust your intuition? Have you had any experiences when you thought if I had just listened to myself? I will share more about how you can strengthen your intuition later in the book.

Self-realisation

By this I mean the faith you have in your higher-self?

Do you believe that you already have all the answers inside of you and that you just need to slow down, get quiet and check in to hear the whispers of your soul?

When your brow chakra is swirling away happily this is exactly what you believe. (If you don't believe it now, you deffo will by the end of this book. I bet you a box of Ferrerro Rocher! (They are my favourite, even though I have a sugar intolerance, shhhhhh!))

Awareness

When your third eye is balanced you allow yourself to take time to reflect and recognise patterns in yourself, others, and your environment.

Questioning the reason why certain things are happening the way they are, and you start to feel into them and understand them, then noticing how you should react to them by how you feel.

Imagination

Allowing yourself to visualise and create your dreams through your imagination. I absolutely LOVE doing this! Closing my eyes and proper daydreaming about the things that I want to bring into my life, then getting all excited about them and peeing glitter everywhere!

I will share more about the power of visualisation later in the book too.

Dreams

When your brow chakra is in alignment you will have more bizarre dreams than ever before, and some may seem like they have messages in them for you? I have the most bonkers dreams. I woke my husband up making the weirdest noises last night because I was screaming in my dream while I was dreaming someone was staring at me through a window and it creeped me out. It apparently means I am feeling self-conscious or have an awareness I am being watched by others. Makes sense.

Have you ever looked up the meaning of your dreams before?

Some of them they will blow your mind.

Clarity

There is not a fluffy bit of brain fog in sight when your third eye is balanced. You will have clarity and be able to make your own mind up about things without looking for external validation, because you just KNOW the answer.

Clear as day! And when the mind is calm it is amazing how quickly, how smoothly and how beautifully you will perceive everything.

Intuition baby. Intuition.

Connection

This is feeling connected to the higher realms. When your third eye is fully open balanced and aligned you can receive messages from angels, spirits, and guides.

This took me years to do but now when I am doing my healing sessions, I am sometimes visited by spirits or guides who have messages for the person I am with. It's amazing! And I still feel a little bit bonkers, but I bloody LOVE IT!

Feeling motivated and having creative energy is another sign that you are aligned. Like having light bulb moments and acting on them, bringing them into reality with clarity instead of just letting them drop in and then float away.

Un-balanced Brow Chakra

When the brow chakra is un-balanced you will experience intense feelings of overwhelm. Feeling like you can't make a decision because there are too many options, you feel confused and are not sure how to find your way out of the brain fog. You will find it hard to concentrate on anything and if you are trying to create something it will feel like you are banging your head against a brick wall. You won't even KNOW what you want to create because clarity will have well and truly left the building.

There can also be a feeling of isolation, where you feel completely disconnected from everything and everyone. Almost like a "what's the point" type feeling as you can't visualise the future. Dark memories of the past creep in and keep you feeling stuck and lost. You have lost your belief in spirit/God/source and in your own ability to perceive things unseen. All your faith has flown out your ear and is nowhere to be seen.

How to rebalance the third eye chakra:

- Meditation and Visualisation.

The most powerful tool that you can use to rebalance the third eye and the crown chakra which we will come to in a moment is meditation and visualisation. A lot of people roll their eyes when you say the word mediation, like you have to be some almost naked bearded guy who has legs that look like a pretzel, levitating off the floor chanting *Om*. Because to be fair for years that's the imagine that has been portrayed.

Recently people have begun to realise that mediation is super easy, can be done anywhere, and has tons of benefits. I resisted meditation for years before I tried it and this was because I thought that meditation meant that you had to sit still and not move for ages while thinking of nothing!

For those of you who know me, know that the squirrels that live in my busy mind are little fuckers, so to me I thought this would be a proper conquest. Anyway, one day I thought fuck it and signed up to be a mediation coach because I don't do anything by halves, the benefits sounded amazing and I thought if I threw myself in at the deep end, I had no choice but to master it.

The transformation was beyond my wildest dreams. I became less reactive, more focused, had more clarity and the ideas, and downloads I was getting were unreal. I also had huge surges where I would release trapped emotion. Out of nowhere mid meditation I would instantly feel sick to the point of thinking I was going to have to leg it the loo, then just before I did, I would be overwhelmed with emotion and sob my heart out uncontrollably for about two minutes. And then it would be gone.

And I would feel so much lighter afterwards.

All meditation really is, is getting comfy, closing your eyes, focusing on your breath, and letting whatever ever comes up for you come up without any judgement or self-sabotaging.

If you feel in the mood you could go back to the beginning of Pillar 1 and do the guided body scan meditation again. Surrender to your soul for 10 minutes and see what happens.

Journal Prompt

Take a few moments to think about if you could take one small step this week that leads you closer to your dreams, what does this step look like? What is your intuition telling you?

Crystals for the Third-eye chakra are:

- Amethyst: Amethyst is a natural tranquiliser, it relieves stress and strain, soothes irritability, balances mood swings, dispels anger, rage, fear, and anxiety. Alleviates sadness and grief, and dissolves negativity. Amethyst activates spiritual awareness, opens intuition, and enhances psychic abilities.
- Azurite: Azurite is known for being a potent psychic stone, shrouded in mystery for centuries its secrets known only to the highest priests and priestesses. It was called the Stone of Heaven by the ancient Chinese who believed it to open celestial gateways. WOW!

It is used to clear away tension and confusion, and opens the mind to new perspectives. This crystal stimulates the intellect, awakening the development of psychic and intuitive abilities, and brings inner vision into alignment with spiritual guidance

The last but definitely not least of the chakras that I am excited to share with you next is the Crown chakra.

22

THE CROWN OF ENLIGHTENMENT

The crown chakra, or sahasrara chakra in Sanskrit, (try to say that after 3 vodkas I dare you!) is known as *the bridge to the cosmos.*

It is the most spiritual in nature of all seven chakras located above the crown of the head, hence known as the crown chakra, it acts as each person's centre of spirit, enlightenment, wisdom, universal consciousness, and connection to higher guidance.

It is our portal to the divine.

I cannot stress how important it is to work on the other six chakras first before this one, as the energy here is supplied by the other lower chakras.

When the crown chakra is activated and balanced you feel like you have found your soul's purpose. You feel enlightened, knowing deeply that we are all connected, and everything is love. You feel that there is no limit to your bliss and that you are in complete control of your mind - a bit like being pissed and not giving a shit - everything is amazing and everything is going to be just fine.

The crown as you may have already guessed is associated with spirituality and connection to your true self. When you develop your crown chakra you become more aware of your conscious self, and how you can bring peace and harmony into your life. You begin to have feelings of interconnectedness and understand that you are not alone, connected to others in spirit.

Some describe this chakra as the gateway to the cosmic self or the divine self, to universal consciousness. When it is aligned it is like being connected to who we are truly meant to be, and we realise that we connected to everyone else too. You make have heard of people being awakened or having a spiritual awakening, this is what it means.

When I am about to do a spiritual healing with a client, I always do a short visualisation to open my crown chakra, so I am open to receiving anything that I need to know or that I need to receive for my client. I close my eyes and bring my awareness to the crown of my head. I breathe in, and as I exhale slowly, I image the top of my head opening like a lotus flower and a beam of beautiful bright white light coming down from the universe and in through the crown of my head.

I feel the warmth of the light enter my body and visualise and feel it going down past my brow, down past my throat, through my heart and my solar plexus, into my sacral and out through my root chakra, cleansing each chakra as the light passes through it. I feel completely connected to the universe then.

I trust myself now, but it took a long time.

Now, I allow my intuition and how my body *feels* to guide me when I receive an intuitive message or messages from a spirit. I used to think I was losing the plot and then I remembered my Reiki master telling me that these things might happen and that the messages weren't for me, so if I didn't understand them that was okay and just to share them with the other person. A bit like Catchphrase. Say what you see.

Almost every time I have done this even when it has seemed like a bonkers thing to say, it has resonated with the other person. And because it has been so random it is something that would have been impossible to make up.

When the crown chakra is blocked:

You may experience feelings of loneliness and being disconnected. By disconnected I mean that you don't have any connection to the higher power, you may have lost faith and no longer believe in the universe or in God, and just cannot seem to get excited about the future as you feel you have no purpose.

Nothing excites you and you feel lost and unsupported but are constantly overthinking everything at the same time.

You may feel like life is just a set of random events that you don't have any control over, so you might as well just plod along. Not believing in anything other than tangible things in life that you can see. Almost like you are completely switching off from any sort of connection and just going through the motions, like a robot with routine.

Another sign that your crown chakra is blocked is that you become strongly attached to material things, like they are all that matter in the world. And that the craving for materialistic things overshadows the desire for the spiritual connection.

You may think that if you can just get a new car then all of your problems will be solved and you will be happy, but when you get the new car, you still feel exactly the same.

Because you are.

Being obsessed with status and achievements but not in regard to personal development or growth for yourself is another alarm bell here. Like you are not working for the greater good and you feel that your status defines who you are, so you NEED the label or the title to show other people this too.

When you feel disconnected there can sometimes be a lot of anger present, like you have been abandoned by the higher powers that be.

And how DARE they do this to you!

You may also find it hard to let go of things that no longer serve you, and you keep harping on about the same thing again and again and again... basically you become a moaning ass.

Ways to balance this beauty:

Again, like the third eye, meditation is at the top of the list here. You can use the visualisation I shared with you above about how I do it to help you feel connected here.

By focusing on loving and helping others you are pushing aside your ego and coming from a place of love instead. Releasing the attachment to the material world and becoming present in the REAL world.

Crystals for the Crown chakra are:

- Clear quartz: Helps with clarity and boosting energy, amazing for assisting with clarity too.
- Selenite: Embodies tranquillity and is highly effective for the advancement of the mind and mental powers.
- Rainbow Moonstone: Brings harmony, balance and hope while enhancing creativity. It strengthens intuition and psychic perception.

I hope that throughout these chapters you have been able to identify areas within yourself that have come to light, and now you know which chakras they are linked to you can begin to nurture and heal yourself from the inside out.

So much shit happens to us in our lives doesn't it? Often, we don't realise what a huge impact things have had on us until our bodies and minds can't take it anymore and begin to try and give us signs that things aren't quite right on an energetic level. Often these are quite unpleasant signs, so we choose to ignore them and pretend they are not happening until sometimes we can't anymore, or we self-medicate and numb the life out of ourselves and go full-on ostrich style plunging our heads into the sand to hide from reality.

I did this for so long, and I wasn't aware that I was doing it until I was forced to stop and look at myself.

Why was I doing these things?

Where had all these thoughts and feelings come from for me to end up getting into this situation? I began to look a bit deeper at what was triggering me and where these triggers had come from.

Join me now as we delve into my Mindset Mastery section, you are deffo gonna need a journal for this bit believe me!

23

PILLAR 2 MINDSET MASTERY

Your mindset and belief system affect everything in your life from what you think and feel to how you act and react to the world around you. When we talk about a person's mindset it is how THEY view the world through their own perspective.

And everyone WILL see things differently, because we have all had a different journey and we all have different opinions and views and ways of thinking about things, so we ARE all looking at life through a completely different lens.

I believe that I had to go through all the dark times and bad experiences to really appreciate how good life can feel. It wasn't easy to change, and it definitely didn't happen overnight, but it was bloody worth it.

When I really dug deep, I found out that there were four main things that had kept me small. They were fear, limiting beliefs, lack of boundaries and comparing myself to other people.

What I also noticed was that discovering these things made me feel a little bit funky at first. Like a bit emotional, and drained and flat and it was for the first time in forever I was seeing the truth and began listening to my own voice and choosing what was right for me.

I did SOOOOO much journaling too, so if you don't have one already, I would suggest you get yourself a notepad and pen for this section so you can see clearly what is coming up for you. Remember that when I say journaling, what I actually mean is dumping every thought that comes into your head, out of your head and onto paper. It doesn't need to be neat or in any sort of order because it's YOURS, just for you and nobody else is going to see it if you don't want them too.

And if you DO write something that you wouldn't want anyone else to see, rip it up, so nobody else can see it.

I am going start with the biggy, the main thing, the most common theme that stops people from doing the things they want to do and it is FEAR!

Fear is one of the most powerful emotions. It has a very strong effect on your mind and your body. Fear can be a positive thing, it keeps us safe, like if we are walking outside at night and we contemplate taking a short cut down an alleyway, fear will kick in and say, "DO NOT EVEN THINK OF GOING DOWN THERE MRS!" so we don't and no baddies jump out on us or kidnap us and we arrive home safely.

Fear can happen at many different times in our lives, but we are going to talk about the fear that holds us back.

Fear feels differently for different people. I want you to think back about something that made you feel scared once and notice where in your body this feeling was? It might show up as a feeling of anxiety across your chest, you might feel it's harder to breathe, it could be a sick feeling in your tummy? Where is yours? It's important to notice this because then when we get this feeling we can see it for what it really is and begin to look deeper into the reasons why it has shown up.

When you feel frightened or seriously anxious, your mind and body work very quickly. These are some of the things that might happen:

- Your heart beats very fast.
- You breathe very fast.
- Your muscles feel weak.
- You sweat a lot.
- Your stomach churns or you feel like you are going to shit your pants.
- You find it hard to concentrate on anything.
- You feel dizzy.
- You feel frozen to the spot.
- You can't eat.
- You have hot and cold sweats.
- You get a dry mouth.
- You get very tense muscles.

These things happen because your body senses fear and prepares you for what could be an emergency. It makes your blood flow super quick to your muscles, spikes your blood sugar, and gives you the mental ability of Einstein on red bull to focus on the thing that your body sees as a threat. You become like a bit of a ninja basically because you are pumped full of adrenalin, ready and waiting to react.

However, fear keeps us in our comfort zone. Our brain will try and stop us doing anything we haven't done before by making us feel scared. This is because when it is something it has not done before it doesn't know what is going to happen, so it shits itself and makes us scared to keep us safe.

But we HAVE to step outside our comfort zones to grow.

If we don't change, we will be stuck with the same routine, the same problems, and the same feelings forever. It is impossible for you to become who you really want to be by staying where you are. Sometimes the place you are used to being, is not the place you belong.

Nothing changes if nothing changes.

We have to take charge of our lives, even if that means quitting the jobs or leaving the people that we have always known to move to something we know will be better for us. To do the things that light a fire in your belly, and make you feel like you want to clench your teeth together and make squeaky noises.

The things that you KNOW will make YOU happy.

The things that you know are worth the risk, even though you are scared. Inaction breeds doubt and fear. Action breeds confidence and courage.

If you want to conquer fear you cannot do it sitting on your ass. GET UP! GET BUSY! DO THE THING!

When we talk about being strong and doing brave things it often gets compared to, "Having balls!" or "Growing a pair of balls!"

But let's take a moment to think about balls. Sorry, yes I am getting you to think about actual testicles right now, but bear with me, I PROMISE there is a method in my madness. Balls are actually very sensitive little things. Well, say little, some of them are quite large aren't they, but anyway! Regardless of size, all they actually do it sit there, and be sensitive and make sperm. I am not saying for one minute that this isn't important, because it definitely is but when being compared in strength, comparing how strong balls are compared to a vagina... vaginas would win hands down!

Vaginas are designed to give birth along with many other functions, but they are most definitely, in my opinion anyway, stronger than bollocks!

So... How did this conversation come about I can hear you asking? It's a little bit random and strange and probably very uncomfortable and even a little bit gross for some people, but here it is. (I have found from sharing this recently that the word vagina makes people feel uncomfortable and even pull a bit of a wincy face, so don't worry if this is also you, it's perfectly normal.)

I was running an online course last year all and was talking to my group about being strong and that how sometimes, even when we are absolutely shitting our pants about doing something that we KNOW we want to do, but fear is standing in our way, for them to embrace this feeling of fear as a positive, knowing that whatever is standing on the other side is going to be AMAZING, we just need to grow a pair...

And then that just didn't feel right, I was visualising these two baggy, soft, unidentical slightly shrivley, hairy balls just dangling there... not making me feel strong AT ALL!

And I was like, "HANG ON!" "NO!" "We need to grow a BIG VAGINA because vaginas are well stronger than balls!"

s where, "Grow a big Vagina" comes from and it makes er chuckle.

What are you scared of?

The most common fear that comes up for my clients is fear of judgement. Fear of what other people think about them. Most of us are people pleasers and this is where the real problem is.

We put other people's feelings before our own because we don't want to offend them or upset them or even make them feel a teeny bit uncomfortable. We would rather swallow all of that ourselves that have someone else feel that way, and often it's people who we don't even know or have no meaning to us.

Have you even gone to do something that made you SOOOO excited and you were about to do it but then this little voice appeared (Inner bitch step forwards please) and said, "They are gonna be thinking "EEEEEEEE, look at her, who does she think she is?" if you do that.

The truth is we create a lot of crazy shit in our heads don't we. Have you ever lay in bed at night and catastrophised or made-up ridiculous stories in your head about what people will say or who might gossip and wanted to put yourself in a box in the cupboard under the stairs? 99% of the time, these things just aren't true.

Sometimes we will hold ourselves in a place of fear by replaying past scenarios in our heads that we just can't let go of and deep down we have a fear of them happening again.

There is a brilliant quote by Theodore Roosevelt:

"It is not the critic who counts; not the man who points out how the strong man stumbles, or where the doer of deeds could have done them better. The credit belongs to the man who is actually in

the arena, whose face is marred by dust and sweat and blood; who strives valiantly; who errs, who comes short again and again, because there is no effort without error and shortcoming; but who does actually strive to do the deeds; who knows great enthusiasms, the great devotions; who spends himself in a worthy cause; who at the best knows in the end the triumph of high achievement, and who at the worst, if he fails, at least fails while daring greatly, so that his place shall never be with those cold and timid souls who neither know victory nor defeat."

I friggin LOVE this!

It explains how some people are quite happy to sit and be Judgey McJudgerson from the side lines and point out the mistakes and poke holes in the things other people who are trying to better themselves are doing but wouldn't even *consider* having a go themselves because they are too scared.

The people who are judging us (or who we think are) have never walked in our shoes. They don't know anything about our lives or what we have been through or what are dreams are?

We cannot change what other people think of us, but we CAN change our views towards the situation. When we change *our* mindset and *our* views and when we *choose* to look at things in a different way then *WE* take the power back over the situation.

So regardless of what others think, we can choose not to be bothered by it, because let's be honest most of the gossipers and whisperers are people who mean nothing to us anyway. Often friends of friends or school mums or people we have just made and aren't even real friends pop up in our delightful little brains. When we can do this, we allow ourselves to come out of our comfort zones, out of our *caves of fear* and start doing the things that SET US FREE, that make us happy.

When we CHOOSE to stop giving a shit about what other people think we become FREE.

AND IT FEELS AMAZING!

When we feel judged, we go through a process. First when the judging happens, we instantly react and defend ourselves, then we internalise what has happened and have a good think about it, (normally dramatising it a bit) and end up with an feeling of unworthiness that we have labelled ourselves.

Have you ever noticed how much you judge other people?

This might feel icky, but allow yourself to go there a minute, there is no self-sabotage, judgement or shame allowed here my beautiful friend, only reflection.

I used to be thee world's worst judger. I was a horror! Looking back it's because the person was triggering me in some way like they were doing the thing that I wanted to do but I wasn't ready or brave enough yet. I would make out the thing they were doing was crap or belittle it and tell myself I didn't need it anyway etc. Or they were saying something that I knew was true but wasn't ready to hear or believe it, because the changes that I would have had to make, and deep down really wanted to, were too hard and I really didn't know where to start or even believe that I could do them.

Is this resonating?

Instead of feeling jealousy and envy and pissed off that you're not doing these things, choose to learn and feel inspired instead. Remember we are all on our own journey, and as my gorgeous

Doris used to say to me all the time, "You are exactly where you are meant to be.".

This is something my mum used to say to me all the time when I was being impatient, and it never used to make any sense.

I was always that person rushing around *Like a blue arsed fly* as she used to say.

Fast forward 20 years and I read an article someone had written that made EVERYTHING make sense. I went from constantly being in a rush and getting pissed off with things that slowed me down, to being able to say in my head, "I am exactly where I am supposed to be." and now I tell everyone who I meet who is in a rush about this story, and I am going to share it with you.

The head of a company survived the 9/11 twin towers tragedy because his son started kindergarten. Another guy was alive because it was his turn to bring in the donuts that day. One woman was late and missed it all because her alarm never went off. One person was late because there had been an accident on the freeway, and he was stuck in traffic. One person missed the bus. One spilled food on her clothes and had to take time to change. One's car wouldn't start. One couldn't get a taxi.

The one that struck me the most was the man who had put on a new pair of shoes that morning. He took various means to get to work, the bus, the train, but before he got there, he developed a huge blister on his foot so he stopped off at a drug store to buy some band aids. That is why he is still alive today.

Now whenever I am stuck in traffic, miss the train, stop to answer the phone or fix my daughters shoe, all the little things that frustrate me because they are slowing me down me, I think to myself... "This is exactly where I am supposed to be at this very moment."

This is one of my most favouritest and most life changing things I have ever read. That little statement, "You are exactly where you are meant to be," just takes all the pressure away of feeling like you should be somewhere or be doing something different than what you are doing right at this moment.

I use it all the time when I feel myself pushing or when something particularly shitty is happening and I have no control over it. I say this to myself and it makes me feel like there is a reason for me to be where I am, doing what I'm doing right at this exact moment. Like all the shit that we have been through has always been for something because we were exactly where we were meant to be, doing what we were supposed to be doing, for some bigger reason that we were ever aware of.

I think, it's kind of nice to believe that life has a little secret journey for us. To be able to surrender to this has been one of the best gifts I have given to myself and during this crazy global pandemic it is what kept me from getting in the cupboard with a bottle of vodka, so much so that when we came out of lockdown I got the word 'surrender' tattooed on my left wrist, to remind me that this is something I always have the power to do.

Something that saved my soul when I was in my darkest time.

Feeling the heaviness and the fear from the whole world as we were all trapped inside. Not knowing what was coming or for how long things would be like this. Surrendering set me free and gave me back some control in my life. I was choosing to let go of trying to change something that I could not. I was choosing to let things unfold as they would and go with the flow of the things that I could not control.

And this allowed me to breathe again.

Everything happens and unfolds exactly as it should and when we can surrender to this instead of rushing through life, EVERYTHING feels so much better.

I believe that we are shown things and cross paths with people in our lives at the exact times that we need them. So now every time I feel like I'm pushing too much and begin to feel out of control, I stop, take a breath, look at the tattoo on my left wrist and remember that we have no control or power over a situation and that we can easily take this back by choosing to surrender.

When we can let go of the things we have no control over, like the recent pandemic for example, and choose to be present about how we are reacting and what we are doing then we don't feel so smothered. At the beginning of lockdown I was a mess. Fear well and truly had hold of me by the labia (I don't have balls, so this seemed appropriate) I felt trapped, controlled, scared, and unbelievably anxious. We were all self-isolating because my son has chronic asthma, so we were told to stay in and not see anyone or go anywhere, it was actually pretty terrifying now I look back.

Mikey had been furloughed and we were all stuck together in the house. At first I didn't know how I was going to cope with us all being in together for so long and began overthinking everything and getting myself in a right flap. Then I realised the only control I had was how *I* reacted to things, so I chose to love us being together and to cherish the time because it was probably never going to happen again. Instead of resisting I surrendered.

I chose the outcome. I chose to love it and we had the best few months ever.

My tattoo reminds me of this every time I look at it. That I get to choose the outcome every time. Sometimes we do get stuck worrying about situations that we can't change. Often it's something from the past that has already happened and we can't' do anything about it, or something from the future that might not ever even happen and we have no control over it!

Don't waste time looking back, you are not going that way, and there is nothing to can do to go back and change anything that has happened, so what's the point in losing time and energy over it!

Do not let yourself be defined by the things that have happened to you, you are NOT your past. Look at the lessons that you have learned from these things. What have they taught you? Choose to take the positive from situations instead of what should have or could have been.

Fear of Failure is another biggy that I hear from my clients. "What if I fail?" they say to me. My answer is always the same. "You can never fail." You always get something from it. And it the words of my beautiful friend Louise, "It's either a lesson or a blessin'"

We always learn something that we would or wouldn't do again from everything we do like the time I cleaned the toaster with a flash wipe and got an electric shock so big it threw me across the kitchen. My lesson was, don't do that again you knob!

I have never done it since.

Often, we fear what people will think of us if we do fail, and I always think have they done the thing we are thinking of doing, or are they going to do it? If the answer is no, then who cares what they think? And if the answer is yes, I normally ask them if I can pick their beautiful brains about how they did and what did and didn't work so I don't make the same mistakes.

Fear of not being good enough is something that I have battled with my whole life, and my inner bitch still whispers it in my ear a couple of times a week but the difference is now I can hear her, whereas before I heard her as MY OWN voice and thoughts, so I believed her.

Little bitch!

We are told our whole lives by society what we should be, do and have. It goes a bit like this.

Go to school, pass exams, go to university, get a good job, meet a partner, get married, go on holidays, have kids, pay off house, work hard your whole life so you have a good pension to retire, live happily ever after. The end.

We are NOT all the same. We are not SUPPOSED to be all the same. There is no cookie cutter for how our lives are supposed to be. But society tells what we SHOULD be on so many levels. And what we should look like too! This massively affects people. People often look outwards for things that they think will make them feel enough, like a new car, a big house, designer clothes or the job with the snazzy title. We are constantly bombarded with images and pressure to be this and look like that. No wonder we are so scared of being ourselves. We don't even know who we are.

THIS NEEDS TO STOP!

There is nobody on this planet like you and that has happened for a reason. Remember my swimmer story from earlier on about there being a 40 trillion quadrillion percent chance that you are gonna be that sperm that meets the egg. And you were!

From all those swimmers, it's US.

It's YOU!

It's ME!

We are here for a reason.

You are unique. You are supposed to be different and be exactly who you are.

You have always been and will always be ENOUGH!

You just need to remember how lucky you are to be here.

Triggers

A trigger is something that sets off an emotional reaction in the form of a memory or flash back related to some kind of trauma. It could be raised voices from being sharply told off as a child, it could be the smell of beer reminds you feeling unsafe around an alcoholic family member, hearing certain words or sayings might remind you of an abusive ex.

Some triggers might not even make sense to anyone but you, that's because we are all so different. Hearing the word Dictator reminds me of my ex. It used to make me feel proper edgy and start my adrenaline spiking through my body.

I don't feel that way anymore because I have done a lot of work on it and the whole situation. And even though in the past I would tell myself to forget it and get over it and that I was being stupid, that initial reaction of fear from that one word was VERY real to me. I felt controlled and trapped, feeling how I felt when I WAS in that situation.

Being told I was not good enough, and that the things I like were ridiculous and people were laughing at me. Being told I was a liar and had done things I hadn't done, like the time he said he had me followed that I mentioned earlier. I was a nervous wreck, he wasn't even having me followed, he was just lying to try and control me from a distance.

The emotions behind a trigger are mainly fear, anxiety, sadness, depression and anger but the real work begins when we are able to specifically identify those emotions that come that make us feel pissed off, feeling upset or scared. When we can do that and really SEE what it is that is making us feel this way, then we can face these triggers and these fears and reassure ourselves that our past trauma is NOT in the present.

Like when I became aware of that word making me feel all these emotions, I could stop and take a minute and comfort myself. Telling myself that I was safe and that it was just a trigger. The key here is to identifying fear noticing when it comes up and being present with it, not distracting yourself or losing your shit, sitting with it and being aware of how and what exactly you are feeling.

Allow yourself to be present and to sit with it. It is OK to have these feelings even though they don't feel good. We have to experience the good and the bad to really appreciate and understand what is happening to us and for us.

Compassion

Showing compassion towards YOURSELF is one of the best ways to help eliminate fear. We all fall off, we all judge ourselves and do a bit of shamey self-sabotage because we are human but what matters is that we forgive this judgement and treat ourselves with love and compassion.

When you show you are compassionate towards yourself, you allow yourself to be vulnerable. Vulnerability does not mean that you are being weak it means that you are choosing to show up and be seen when you have no control over the outcome. Therefore, being vulnerable means you are showing that you are in fact strong.

There is an amazing quote by one of my favourite ever authors Brene Brown about vulnerability:

"Vulnerability is the birth place of love, belonging, joy, courage, empathy and creativity. It is the source of hope, empathy, accountability and authenticity."

It is so important that you realise that being your authentic self is where your true magnificence lies. Like I said before, there is only one YOU. Your willingness to let the world see you in your truth is your greatest gift.

When you let people see the true you, even at your darkest moments, they really connect to you. Showing yourself to be imperfect is the most refreshing and comforting thing you can do in my opinion. When we can lock our egos away and stop pretending that we have all the answers it takes the pressure off us massively and shows the other person that we are relatable and just like them.

Sometimes even if you can't put your finger on the exact emotion that you are feeling, just by saying, "I am uncomfortable," is enough for you to accept that something is going on. Then give yourself permission to sit with it. No judgement. No criticism. Notice your self-talk. How would you speak to a child who felt this way? Remember however you are feeling is always ok. All feeling matter exactly the same way, we are just often taught as children that some are bad and some are good.

But YOU get to decide.

You ALWAYS have a choice how to react.

Becoming self-aware is the key.

24

WHETHER YOU THINK YOU CAN OR YOU THINK YOU CAN'T YOU'RE RIGHT

Limiting beliefs - what are they? (Apart from a pain in the ass!)

False beliefs we hold about ourselves - they restrict us and inhibit us and generally make us feel miserable.

"I can't wear that dress I'm too overweight!"

I'm not as qualified as the other people in this meeting, I can't speak up."

A limiting belief is any sentence that starts with:

- I must
- I can't
- I am not
- I don't
- I should
- I shouldn't

They hold us back from doing things because we incorrectly believe that we can't or we shouldn't do some of the things that we want to do and so these things exist unquestioned in our minds.

We simply accept them as rules we should live by. We BELIEVE these things to be true, when in fact *truth* and *belief* are two completely different things.

Beliefs don't need proof or require evidence and rely on trust, faith and having confidence in something or somebody.

Truth is based on facts and evidence. Truths can be verified as real and certain and cannot be argued with.

Some beliefs are there to keep us safe, like we don't touch the cooker because we believe we will be burned, this is based on the truth.

However, this is NOT the case with limiting beliefs.

Limiting beliefs are constructed from our past experiences, often shaped and formed through childhood at an early age, these beliefs are naïve, misinformed, shrouded in inaccuracy and usually wrong.

They are not truths.

They are not the factual entity that we perceive them to be, because our little brains were immature when they were formed. But despite this we treat them as if they are gospel, and we accept them without question.

Sadly, they can have a devastating effect on our lives. They hold us back and cause us to make inaccurate judgements and they stop us from enjoying our lives.

And guess what. We ALL have them!

We hold them about ourselves, our relationships and the world in general. These beliefs guide us. We follow their rules and we do not question their validity. We hold beliefs about what we are able to accomplish, the rights we have, the permissions we have and about what we are allowed to do.

This was the biggest one for me, being ALLOWED!

My old business coach once said something to me, and it was like a massive lightbulb! I really wanted to do something, but I was scared and worried that I wasn't qualified enough to start my mindset coaching programme and she said, "You don't need permission!"

BING!

I felt like I was watching heavy shackles being unlocked from my body and turning into butterflies that fluttered off into the sky.

I WAS allowed to do whatever I wanted.

I didn't need permission. It was all in my head the things that I was telling myself about not being good enough or qualified enough and what people would think.

It was all bollocks.

Limiting beliefs are commonly formed in childhood and our teenage years and are products of our experiences. However, a significant experience at any point in our lives can create a new limiting belief.

Our limiting beliefs are based on a complex body of evidence that sits beyond our frame of consciousness. In other words, we might never be able to explain why we accept that some of our limiting beliefs are true.

Are you ready for some more science?

There is a very clever part of our brain called the RAS (Reticular Activating System). This little beauty is like the refence library of our brains. It is where every experience that happens leaves an impression which is then processed and stored in this place.

For example, I fell over when I didn't tie my shoelaces = I must tie my shoes laces or I will fall over.

The RAS is amazing at recalling and filtering information, it's like when we are going to buy a new white Renault, it's the only car we see on the roads. They are suddenly EVERYWHERE!

The RAS hums along quietly in the background, providing us with all the info we need on demand. However, the RAS is incredibly compliant. If we think that we are a failure, the RAS will kick into action and provide us with ALL the information and evidence that we need to conclusively prove this belief. The RAS seeks information that validates your beliefs. It filters the world through the perimeters you give it, and your beliefs shape those perimeters.

For example, if you think you are bad at giving speeches, you probably will be. If you think you can do it without breaking into a sweat and going illuminous purple, you will most probably do that too. The RAS will help you see what you want to see and in doing so will influence the action that you take. This is an even bigger reason WHY it is so important to monitor and be very aware of our thoughts.

Beliefs as Children

From being born as tiny humans up to the age of seven years old, our brains are like little sponges. We soak up all the information we can get our hands on and ask 476738 questions a day without doubting any of the answers from the people who are telling us *their* version of the truth.

As kids we believe truths from our parents such as Santa Claus and the Easter Bunny are real, you can't leave food and as kids we take things at face value, especially what our parents tell us, we believe them without question. After all, why would they lie to us?

Another thing we don't question is rules from authority and sometimes these are not even true or fair.

As kids we are often fed inaccurate information which is then filtered by an immature mind and stored in the RAS, leaving a lasting impact. For example, a bad experience we have had as a kid where we tried to make a friend one day and someone was mean to us and told us to go away, this would have a lasting impact on us as it is stored in the RAS that one time when we tried to make a friend it was really scary. So, we don't do it again, because every time we THINK about making a friend our brain plucks out this negative experience.

Instead, we wait for people to come and speak to us and grow up a shy, withdrawn adult. Considering we are sophisticated creatures, it's amazing how we make decisions based on very little factual evidence.

Social Fear

This is something that held me back for a long time. The thought of being laughed at, judged or criticised is a powerful, unhelpful demotivator.

Too often we don't take the risk because we are certain there will be scary consequences and sometimes when we fail at something we use this to stay small, and not to do the thing again or even try again. (These are excuses by the way!)

How to Identify Limiting Beliefs

We will often start the sentence with:

I can't... speak in public...

I must / mustn't...show my emotions...

I am not... Good enough to...

I should... visit my parents more...

I shouldn't ...eat that bar of chocolate or "ll get fat...

Everyone has their own version of these.

We often believe people are better than us too. "The Jones are the perfect family, they never argue, and their house is always spotless." But we don't actually see behind closed doors, we only see what The Jones want us to see.

Often we believe that we will never be successful in certain situations. Like "I will never get a loan" or " I will never get that job." So we don't bother applying and we miss out on so many opportunities.

As we go through life believing our limiting beliefs, we adapt them into our adult lives. Here are a few examples:

- Belief: I am not loved

In adult life we will become a people pleaser with a desire to be liked at all costs, and often giving too much of ourselves away.

- Belief: I am lazy/no good/Useless compared to others

This can show itself in adulthood as perfectionism. The need for everything to be just so, and always having to be busy doing some sort of tidying or sorting out because if we sit down and relax people will think we are lazy and no good. This was something I used to do all the time, my mum used to say to me, "Can't you just bloody sit down and relax!" But I couldn't, I had so much nervous energy because I believed that I wasn't good enough and that relaxing meant I was wasting time because I had so much I could be doing.

- Belief: I am weak if I show my emotions

This is a bit of a dangerous limiting belief as if we go into adulthood believing that showing our emotions is a weakness, and that weakness is bad, then we can become withdrawn and closed off. Also, if we are feeling emotional or experiencing stress in our lives and we bottle it up this can be detrimental to our health.

There are so many others, but you get the idea here.

Once you realise the actual impact that these limiting beliefs can have or have had on your life it is perfectly okay if feelings of anger, sadness, regret, or shock come up.

We can feel like we have been lied to because people may have told us things that we just believed and took as gospel without questioning them. Sometimes this is what these people have been told too, but they never questioned them either. It's okay if strong feelings come up around this but what you need to remember here is that you now have the choice to change these things moving forwards.

How can you overcome limiting beliefs?

Be willing to challenge yourself. What are you gaining form holding onto this belief? Finding what is called the perceived value in your story is the real game changer here.

Say for example you decide you want to change your job, but you have a BIG ASS belief that you won't be successful if you apply. Ask yourself, "How does this belief help you, and what do you gain by holding onto it?"

By staying in your job, you believe that there will be no disruption to your life, and you won't feel worried or uncomfortable being the newby and beginning a new role. But in the long run is this beneficial?

Absolutely NOT!

Because the reason you want to get a new job is the one you have now is not bringing you any joy or satisfaction in your life, there is no chance of progression either so you will never be able to make any more money. It's easier to stay than go through all the initial stress and discomfort of getting a new job, so you decide you will stick to the story that you might not be successful and stay where you are.

Get Uncomfortable

We do not grow from a place of comfort. As humans we are programmed to leg it in the other direction when we experience discomfort. It is easier to quit when fear, self-doubt and limiting beliefs show their face. JUST SIT WITH IT! It is perfectly ok to feel this way. You need to get used to having these feelings of discomfort if you are ever going to make any changes in your life. Instead of labelling them as negative feelings, sit with them and embrace them for all that they are. What do you need to do for yourself that can help you with this feeling? Self-love perhaps.

Fear stands in front of all the amazing things that we want, so know that when fear shows up and you feel like you want to shit your pants, this means you are on the right path and is normally an indication that something amazing is about to happen.

Change the nervous or scared feeling to excited butterflies instead, both feel exactly the same, we just need to remember to choose.

Journal Prompt

Write down where you are not happy in your life.

Now write down the limiting beliefs that have caused you to get there or are keeping you stuck in that situation.

Now write down the type of reality you want to create. What kind of beliefs does this version of you who lives in this reality have?

How would this version of you live out these beliefs? How would you act, speak, interact with others, walk into a room? What kind of decisions would you make?

What can you choose to believe today to align you with the reality you want to create?

Being Present

When we are present, we can catch our inner bitch when she is chatting shit to us. Being present is one of the best ways to notice this happening. When our inner bitch steps forward she often does so quietly at first and whispers in our ear. Increasing the volume of her words until they become so loud, they completely consume and overpower us.

When you notice the feelings you are having in your body when this happens, the tight chest, shortness of breath, feeling numb, losing concentration, feeling sick, STOP what you are doing and bring your awareness to your breath. Slow it down.

Is what is being said true? NOT a belief? TRUE? Is it kind? Did it need to be said? How can we make it better by changing the words we are using towards ourselves?

Words have power. They can destroy and create. We need to choose to use this force constructively with words of encouragement, instead of words of destruction. Words have their own energy and power with the ability to heal, to help, to hinder, to harm, to humiliate and to be humble. Think back to the water experiment with Dr Emoto, where even negative thoughts and intentions affected the structure of the water. We need to be very selective with the words we choose whoever they are for.

Change your ways

Instead of seeing change as scary or impossible think of it as new and exciting. Notice how you feel, fear and excitement feel the same we just need to choose which one we want to feel. They key here is being present, noticing the dialogue and changing it up.

Remember things take time and it's okay if sometimes we let things slip. We just have to keep going. It takes twenty-one days to make or break a habit so the more we do it the more of a habit the positive words and excitedness is going to become.

Stop saying sorry

When I first met Mikey, this was the word that I said the most. I used to say, "Sorry would you like a cup of tea?" And he would be like, "Why are you sorry?" I was unbelievably submissive and sorry was in all of my sentences. They didn't make sense.

By saying sorry we are telling people that we don't believe in ourselves, that we don't believe what we are doing is right or true, so we are apologising for our behaviour.

I notice language a lot now when people are talking to me. And if someone says sorry and it's not necessary, I will always say to them, "You have no reason to be sorry…".

What I have also started doing is saying thank you instead of sorry. Now if I am late meeting someone, instead of saying, 'Sorry I'm late!" I will say, "Thank you for waiting for me."

Try it and notice how different it feels, it really does change everything.

Stop Comparing

There is nothing positive to be gained from worrying about how you compare to others.

There is a well know quote by President Theodore Roosevelt "Comparison is the thief of Joy", and it is 100% truth.

When we compare ourselves with what others have or simply how they are, we are essentially setting ourselves up to feel inadequate and deflated. With social media being a readily available platform for people to flaunt every aspect of their lives, there are high expectations to own the latest material things, look a certain way or earn a certain amount of money. It is only inevitable that we as humans are going to get sucked right into that trap.

It is so important to base your expectations on what YOU do and your own dreams, not what others are doing. When we try to follow in the path of others and start to believe that their dreams are our dreams, we instantly lose our sparkle or vision and our smile.

Remember your why!

What are your reasons for doing the things that you want to do?

What do your dreams mean to you and why are they so important?

Stay in your lane. I have a picture above my desk that says, "You Do You!" and every time I look at it, it reminds me that there is only one me.

Sometimes we see people who are successful and happy and are all over Instagram and Facebook doing their thing that seems like the best thing ever so you decide, 'I'm gonna do that thing too.". But that thing is THEIR thing, and the thing that makes THEM happy and sparkle all over the place may very well switch your right off.

I have a beautiful friend who is a very successful lawyer. She has studied law her whole life and is now on social media sharing her beautiful holidays and her exquisite lifestyle because her business is doing amazing and by the way she bloody deserves everything. If I thought for one minute that being a layer would make me happy then I am clearly deluded. Anything rules related, policies, procedures or where numbers are concerned by brain puts its fingers in its ears and starts singing, "lalalalalalalalala!" Instantly switched off.

I cannot compare myself to her because we are totally different, so I choose to send her love and admiration and feel into her success with her. Feeling grateful that one day soon I will have my own version of this too. But it will be MY OWN!

I want you to remember that YOU are so bloody special. Everything about you is beautifully unique and I want you to remember that you are good enough exactly as you are.

When comparisionitis creeps in, our inner bitch is normally not far behind. She comes to remind us how inferior we are compared to that other person and how we will never be that successful, beautiful, happy, you fill in the blank here.

By choosing to feel happy for this other person we are admiring, we take away the need to pull ourselves down and by feeling into this feeling of happiness and excitement for them and imagining it for ourselves too, we are raising our vibration and starting to attract this into our own lives by showing the universe that we also are ready for a piece of this.

Journal prompt

I have a little exercise for you. I want you to write a list of all the things that you love about yourself and your life.

I know this might feel a little bit squirmy and weird at first but when you become aware of all the great things you have going for yourself, you will feel instantly uplifted.

Ask yourself what makes you and your life different? And I want you to acknowledge everything here, how you look, how you laugh, your sense of humour, your values, the fact that you have amazing friends, do you have a talent that nobody else can do?

There is no limit to how long this list can go so just go for it and see how positive it makes you feel. You may want to keep this list somewhere you can grab it next time you start comparing yourself to other people.

Don't spin too many plates

Sometimes when we already have a lot of plates spinning and people ask us to do something, the people pleaser in us really wants us to add that extra plate, because what difference will one more make?

When we keep adding and taking on little extra bits here and there what we are really doing is setting ourselves up to fail. When you begin to feel the stretch ask yourself, "Can I realistically achieve this?" And if you FEEEEEEEEL the stretch and you don't think you can then you are only setting yourself up to fail. When we say yes and take on too much and then fail, our self-confidence and self-belief take a proper nosedive.

It is okay to say *No* but I will be covering this in more detail as I know this is something a lot of people find very difficult. This used to be me all over. Saying *No* used to make me feel all squirmy and uncomfortable inside.

Don't worry I got you.

Journal Prompt

So now you know what they are, I would love for you to take some time out and write down anything that has come up for you around this.

I am going to talk to you in this next section about something that I never had in my life until I was about 38.

But OH MY GOD as soon as I discovered Boundaries and how important they are I put them in my life all over the friggin' show. This is something that changed my life and I am excited to share it with you.

25

NO IS A COMPLETE SENTENCE

Never heard of a boundary? Neither had I.

I used to make decisions based on what would please other people rather than myself. I used to say, "Yes" to things that I really, really, really, did NOT want to do, even when every little cell in my body was screaming "NOOOOOOOOO!" then I would lie in bed at night totally pissed off with myself for not saying what I actually thought or felt and would cry hot tears until I eventually fell asleep.

I had absolutely NO boundaries in my life until about three years ago. I had never even heard of a boundary let alone understood what one was.

If you look in the dictionary the word *boundary* means 'a line'. The boundaries I am referring to are the boundaries that people cross and take the piss out of us, because they know we don't have any either. They completely (and sometimes unintentionally) take advantage of our good nature.

A personal boundary is an imaginary line that separates me from you. Separates my physical space, feelings, needs and responsibilities from yours and other peoples. Boundaries allow you to be your true self. They create a separation that allows you to have your own feelings, make your own decisions and ask for what you want without needing to please others. Does this sound a bit like the impossible right now? Don't worry it did to me too.

Here's a question, how can you be your true self when you don't even know who you are? You may never have thought about what YOU like because you have just aimed to please other people your whole life?

Does walking on eggshells feel like the daily norm to you as you try to say and do the right things so that you don't upset anyone or cause any sort of conflict? This used to be me.

Is this resonating?

Journal prompt

Take a moment to brain dump on this and see what comes up for you? Do you have boundaries? If not, who do you need them from and why?

Remember these are your words, you can't get it wrong, just dump all the thoughts from your head onto a piece of paper. That's it.

I now realise that boundaries are an important and an essential form of self-care. Healthy emotional boundaries mean that you value your own feelings and needs and that you are not responsible for how others feel or behave. Boundaries allow you to let go of worrying about how others feel, and places accountability squarely back with them. Ever heard the saying, "That's your shit not mine!" this is where that would come in.

When we can tell people clearly what our boundaries are, they know how they are expected to behave. This is easier said than done, especially if you have put up with something for a long time and are now trying to implement changes within a relationship where the other person is clearly happy taking the piss out of you.

When we don't express our expectations to people, and they continue to take the piss we begin to feel resentment and anger towards them. It's like we really want to tell them to stop but we are too scared of the consequences, so we don't, and things just stay the same and then we feel really pissed off and angry towards the person because they just carry on being a knob end. But they might not actually KNOW that they are being a knob end because we haven't told them, so carry on being annoying and upsetting and taking the piss.

This is why it is sooooooooo super important to tell people as soon as we feel this way.

Boundaries create safety by keeping out what feels emotionally and physically uncomfortable. All relationships need boundaries as without them people won't know what is acceptable and what isn't so, like I just said above, they may take advantage of you because you haven't set limits about how you expect to be treated.

Here is an example.

Meet Chris.

Chris is an elderly gentleman who lives on his own in a little bungalow. Chris's pride and joy is his beautiful garden. It is surrounded by lush green hedges and has a gate with a mailbox at the end of the long path leading to his house. Every day, Chris takes a slow stroll down to his mailbox, admiring his beautiful petunias and roses. He collects his newspaper and slowly strolls back to the house where he sits, by the window, where he can see his flowers, reading his paper. Loving life.

One day, there is a knock at Chris's door. It's very early and he wonders who it is? He answers the door to find a woman in her late twenties standing there with a newspaper in her hand.

"Hiya!" She says, "I have just moved in next door and was passing so thought I would bring you your paper!"

Chris is a bit taken back, but just says, "Oh thanks!" and takes the paper.

"No worries, have a good day!" says the woman and makes her way down the path. Just before she gets to the gate, she picks a flower and then leaves the gate wide open.

Chris feels a little bit of rage flare up, but just does a big sigh and makes his way down the path to close the gate.

The next day there is a knock at the door again. Chris answers the door and finds the woman standing there again with his paper and a crying child.

"Hiya, here's your paper love!" she chirps as she shoves the paper towards Chris and promptly turns on her heels dragging the screaming child down the path. Just before they get to the gate she stops and shows the child the beautiful flowers. The woman then tells the child to pick some to stop it from crying, and they leave without closing the gate!

Chris is so mad he has just done a little bit of sick in his mouth and feels like he wants to drop kick the woman and the child out of his garden, had they not already left. He is furious!! But still doesn't say anything.

Que day three where there is a knock at the door. Chris winces as soon as he hears it, fearing what he is going to be met with this time.

"Morning love, here's ya paper!" says the woman, who this time has two children fighting with her and a DOG!

She pokes the paper under Chris's arm and turns to shout at the kids. "Get out now ya little bastards, what have I told you!" The kids are pushing and shoving each other so much that one of them falls into his prize petunia bush! The woman drags the kid out of the bush, which is now mangled and flat, as she turns to leave she shouts at the dog to follow her. Which it does, after it has finished taking a big dump on Chris's grass. And then they all leave... and leave the gate open!

The top of Chris's head now bursts open, and flames blaze out with fury and anger! His blood is boiling, and he is FURIOUS! He hates the woman, he hates the kids, he hates the dog, he hates that she has moved in next door! Chris storms inside, rips his newspaper to shreds and slams the front door closed.

Now, let's just take a look at this situation here. From the outset it may appear that this woman has took the piss, and in all fairness, she has been pretty disrespectful. However, it is up to Chris to set the boundaries here. He has neglected to do it and has let the woman to continue to collect his paper for him every day.

The woman did not know that Chris didn't want her to collect his paper, she thought she was doing something kind. She also didn't know that Chris like the walk down his garden each day to look at his prize petunias, which she picked and then her kid flattened!

The point is, when you don't speak up and SAY a boundary has been crossed it gives the impression that you are okay with what has happened. It is always better if you say from the start that you are uncomfortable with something.

Chris could have said, "Thanks for thinking of me, but please don't move my paper as I like to collect it myself so I can walk down the garden and look at my flowers. Also please don't pick my flowers as they are my award-winning petunias."

When a boundary is crossed, we need to provide feedback saying that it is not ok. We also need to tell the person why it's not okay or they won't understand why. Sometimes a consequence may be needed as certain toxic people will continue to challenge it.

If for example Chris's neighbour didn't stop after he had told her and just kept coming in the garden, Chris could get a sign on the gate saying, 'DO NOT ENTER!". Or if that didn't work, a lock for the gate. And then if that didn't work, perhaps a super soaker or a catapult.

What stops us from setting boundaries?

Are you a people pleaser?

For the most of us it is that we are people pleasers. We are scared of what the other person will say or how they will feel if we set a boundary. We can be this way for many different reasons which I will talk about over the next few pages.

But for now, here's a fab little exercise that you can do if you know you need to set a boundary but are scared of what will happen.

Journal Prompt

Write down both outcomes. On one side of a piece of paper write down what will happen if you do set the boundary, like you will feel less criticised and able to speak your truth more.

And then on the other side write down what will happen if you don't, so could be you will continue to feel frustrated and overtalked and unhappy.

This will help to give you more confidence and feel certain that you are doing the right thing.

You don't know how to set a boundary

If you have grown up in a family without boundaries, you probably never saw anyone model or teach you healthy boundaries. I grew up in a house with my grandparents where my nan was a bully. If she wasn't happy then nobody was, and everyone did everything within their power to make sure she was. We weren't allowed boundaries where she was concerned as the whole world revolved around her. If her feathers got ruffled then by god we knew about it. For days, or even weeks sometimes. She could hold a grudge for years that woman. And she DID!

Low Self worth

Some part of you feels unloved, therefore you always struggle to prove your worth by putting other people's needs before your own. You are not used to being treated with respect, so you don't even know what it looks like.

People pleasing (Again)

When we haven't had boundaries before, setting boundaries can disrupt our relationships. You will almost definitely get resistance, but it becomes easier as you gain confidence that what you are doing is the right thing.

If we have never told a person that what they are doing or have always done is suddenly not okay anymore, this will make them naturally question us and they will very often resist this because most people don't like change, and because we were probably making their lives soooooo much easier by doing things for them and if we stop it now means they have to do it for themselves and they won't like that much.

Sometimes we THINK it is going to be really bad when actually, it ends up being fine.

There are boundaries that we can set with ourselves too, things like:

- Limiting screen time – this is one of mine.
- Not working past 7pm – this is also one I need.

- Sticking to your budget.
- Only buying what is on your shopping list – yep this is mine too.
- No more than one takeaway a week – (is two ok?)
- Not drinking through the week.

How to set boundaries:

- Be clear on what you want. There is no point trying to speak with someone if you are not able to articulate what you want exactly, it will just make things even more complicated.
- Be direct and don't apologise. Don't pussy foot around. Tell the person kindly but straight, and don't say sorry for wanting to change things that probably shouldn't have ever happened in the first place.
- Expect resistance and don't let it put you off. Don't delay speaking with someone because you know there may be a little bit of a battle. Stand your ground and be kind but firm and clear on what you want to say.
- Practise in the mirror of that helps first. You might feel a bit nobby but it really helps saying it out loud first and pre-empting any come backs you may need. If you know the person well, you can normally get a good idea what they are going to say.
- Remember setting boundaries is an on-going process. It's not something that once it is done you will never have to do it again. Once you have done it once and feel the benefits, it is something that will become a massive part of your self -care.
- Always set boundaries for your own wellbeing, NEVER to control others. Because that's just mean.

How to say No without feeling guilty

The thought of saying *No* to someone used to make me physically feel sick. The reasons I felt this way was because I had no confidence, which made me feel guilty, and I felt guilty because I was a people pleaser.

Saying no to others means we are saying yes to ourselves.

Most women are raised to be good girls and be good for other people. In the past we were taught that our value as a human being comes from how much we help or serve others, not how much we personally grow or achieve. It is therefore a learned trait to say *Yes* to everyone else's wants, needs, problems etc. because that is what is means to be a good woman.

Which creates this MEGA anxiety inside of us that we HAVE to say *Yes* to everything asked of us no matter how much we want to say no.

When we take on too much and spin too many plates, they eventually come crashing down around us. Then we feel worthless and not good enough because despite how hard we tried we still couldn't do it. But the truth is, nobody could.

We can learn to break this negative habit by prioritising ourselves a bit more, and this will then stop all of this happening. Know your worth. You are just as worthy as these other people to have happiness and balance in YOUR life too.

Notice our Gut reaction

If your initial reaction isn't a definite YES with bells on, then it should always be a NO.

Your time is too precious my beautiful one to be doing stuff you don't want to do. Now is the time to pluck up the courage and stand up for what you want. The thing to remember here is if you say yes to this, what are you going to miss out on? What are the other things you could be and would most definitely rather be doing?

HOW to say No

Here are some examples of how to say no:

- I am grateful to have this opportunity, but unfortunately, I can't commit at this time but thank you for thinking of me.
- Thank you so much for thinking of me, but I am not going to be available because of ...insert reason...I hope it all goes well and I will be thinking of you.
- I'm busy that day already doing ...
- I'm already booked.
- No thanks, it's not really my thing, but I hope you all have a fab time.
- I'm not available that date.

Try and remember that 99% of the time nobody will be mad at you for saying no. If you have a circle of kind, caring people who want what is best for you too, they will be happy that you have put yourself first.

However, if you do have toxic people in your lives there are a few ways that you can avoid them. Distance yourself gradually, you are allowed to NOT answer the phone, the door, the message. You don't ever have to feel guilty about removing toxic people from your life.

It doesn't matter whether that someone is a relative, romantic interest, employer, childhood friend or a new bestie – you do not have to make room for people who cause you pain or make you feel small.

It is one thing if the person owns up to their behaviour and makes the effort to change, but if a person disregards your feelings or ignores your boundaries and continues to treat you in a harmful way, they really have to go.

Know that you deserve to say YES to yourself. Your worth as a human is MORE than how you show up for other people. The only one who gets to decide your worth is YOU. It doesn't come from how much you have in the bank or how many friends you have. It doesn't come from someone else's opinion of what you are worth, it comes from being yourself and being proud of who you are.

It's called *self-worth* for a reason, because it comes from you.

It comes from being that person that you can rely on and someone that you love. All the other stuff will change with time, but who you are deep inside of your meat suit, that gorgeous sparkling soul of creativity, kindness, strength, and compassion, THAT is where your worth comes from.

You matter.

Your life matters.

Your hopes and dreams and desires matter.

And you have always, always, always been enough!

Journal Prompt

Take a few minutes to reflect on what things look and feel like for you in your life right now.

Write down any areas where you can see you need to insert a boundary.

Write down what is holding you back.

Now write down what you can do to take steps to overcome these things and things you can do towards making them happen.

This Mindset Mastery section is all of the things that have helped me to understand what was going on inside my head, and how most of the time I was chatting absolute bollocks to myself. I hope it will help you to master your own mindset too.

The next pillar of my programme is all about The Law of Attraction. Here I will help you to get crystal clear about what you want in your life, why you want it and to show you how to activate the gifts of the universe to create abundance in your life.

To uncover and discover your goals, visions, and dreams to start your own journey towards your dream life.

26

PILLAR 3 THE LAW OF ATTRACTION - ASK, BELIEVE, RECEIVE

Now THIS is what REALLY makes me pee glitter!

I stumbled across the Law of Attraction a few years ago when I heard about the book *The Secret*, and within a week it had been given to me by a friend.

It's like it came on my radar, fell into my sub-conscious shopping basket, and arrived on my lap JUST LIKE THAT!

The Law of Attraction is a universal law that states what you put your attention on GROWS! It's all about manifestation. You attract to you what you what you believe, feel, and think about continuously. The pre-steps to the manifesting bit are to recognise this and get very, VERY clear and deliberate about what you have been thinking.

The LOA isn't just about thinking about something and it suddenly appearing, you need to get very, very clear.

Let's use the example of wanting a new car. You want a new car. You have had enough of the one you have, and it feels a bit old and bits have started to go wrong with it, so you decided you are going to manifest yourself a new car.

"I want a new car!" you say out loud.

There, done! The universe knows I want a new car, and I'm not bothered what I get but I just want a new car. In your head you just keep thinking about a new car. Nothing specific. Just a new car, not being greedy so will wait and see what I get from the universe. Then, the clutch on your car goes suddenly. You have no money to get it fixed so you end up having to scrap your car and get a new car with the money you got for your car.

TADA! Say's the Universe "There is your NEW car!"

And you're like, "But I wanted a NEWER car than the one that I had, not an old banger!"

And the universe replies "But you never said!"

Are you with me here?

The first rule of the Law of Attraction is that unless you are CLEAR about what you want, the universe may still deliver but it won't be what you had expected.

Let's look at this again.

Say you said to the universe this time that you wanted a new car, and it was a cherry red BWM 8 series. The interior was black leather and it smelt like vanilla from the sparkly unicorn magic tree that was hanging on the rear-view mirror. Two weeks later you win a competition you entered for this exact car in a magazine.

"TADA!" goes the universe, "Here is your new car!"

"Thank you!" you say.

Now see what I mean by clear.

But how do I GET clear I can hear you asking?

OK so what if you don't know what you want?

How to create a clear vision of how you want to live your life and what you want to achieve, have, be, do...

When we get clear we can really start to focus on attracting and manifesting what we want. It's ok to NOT know the answer to this question. Please be assured that most people have no idea, or at least think they don't.

Getting clear on what you truly want is THEE most important step to realising your dreams and making changes in your life.

There are a few key areas that we need to focus on when getting clear. When we tidy up our lives, we can begin to get clear, and there are so many things we need to keep track of now more than ever before, this can be a lot trickier than it sounds.

Sometimes we can read all the different articles about how to get more organised and what to do, but it can all just feel overwhelming. We buy the notice board and all the stationary and have all these good intentions and then get really pissed off with ourselves when we don't actually know where to start.

And some of us aren't born naturally organised people (I just raised my hand) so it's important to try and build habits into our lives. (Is anyone familiar with the word procrastination? Most days I am the procrastination queen.)

It can make us feel overwhelmed with the number of tasks and list upon lists that we need to complete, and all the other responsibilities in our lives. How are we ever meant to discover our purpose and follow our dreams when we feel out of control in our lives?

Here are some simple steps:

De-clutter your environment

When you have a cluttered, messy, and un-organised environment it is completely de-motivating. Do you feel like you can get stuff done when you are sitting in a room full of mess?

Before I start anything, I HAVE to have a clean, clear table and be able to see out of my back room window. The back of our house is elevated because we live on a hill and our back window looks out over other houses. On a clear day in between the two houses opposite we can see the Welsh hills. I am looking at them right now and they are the most beautiful hazey purply colour.

But if the table is full of last night's placemats and bits of old rice and crumbs and Daisy's baby doll nappies it TOTALLY DISTRACTS ME! I always make sure that the night before, I tidy up and then I know in the morning, when I come down, I can do the things that I want without getting distracted and having to tidy up and getting all pissed off about it first thing in the morning. It's DONE!

I wake up come downstairs, put the kettle on, do my meditation, make my lemon water and crack on!

You may be looking around your home right now thinking, "Fuckin'ell I have more than a kitchen table to de-clutter. THIS IS OK. Do not let this stress you out.

My old boss used to say, "How do you eat an elephant?" "One bite at a time!" Meaning if you have a big job to do, do it a bit at a time. One cupboard or one room at a time. Then when it's done it should be so much easier to keep clean and tidy, instead of turning the whole house upside down and never getting anything done.

Start with the places you use the most and keep those areas clean. Try not to let things get so massy and unorganised again that you find it hard to keep on top of.

I can totally hear the peeps with small humans mouthing, "Yeh right!" and I totally get it! All I am saying here is do what you can to create space in the places you need them, whatever that looks like for you. Don't stress yourself over it.

A good rule to have before you buy anything new is that you have to get rid of something old, that way you stop buying things you don't really need and creating more clutter.

Have a daily Brain Dump

Same as de-cluttering your environment, you must also de-clutter your mind.

I don't know about you, but my brain goes a million miles a second most days. When I wake up it's like "HEY THERE! SO, I HAVE BEEN THINKING..." like it's been waiting all night for me to wake up. My hubby goes mad at me some nights, because I just verbally brain dump all over him while he is trying to get to sleep and waffle away to him.

When there are too many thoughts and ideas on all of the different tasks and responsibilities and to do lists you need to complete, your mind is overwhelmed, and this will only stop you from making progress.

So have a brain dump. Get it allllllllll out.

Dump it all. Absolutely everything. You can do it on paper, on your computer as a voice note whatever suits you. I like to write it out on a piece of paper. Sometimes I like to do little doodles and circle things and write things that make me excited REALLY BIG!

We naturally overthink things when they remain in our heads. They start off as a small little brain fart, then we think about them some more which makes them grow bigger and eventually they are fookin' mahooisve and so much bigger and scarier than they actually are.

By writing it down and getting it out of your head you can LOOK at it on the paper and SEE that it's not actually that scary after all. We just let it turn from a tadpole to an elephant within such a short time and then shit ourselves and lose the plot.

If you can, start the week with a huge brain dump and then each day or a few times throughout the day, do mini daily dumps. I have to do these all the time because I honestly am like the dog of the film Up. Doug gets distracted by squirrels and loses his chain of thought all the time, and that is exactly me. If I don't write the idea down straight away it floats out my head like a little fluffy cloud never to be seen again.

We lose so many good ideas this way.

Get a Journal or Diary

We cannot rely on our squishy little brains to remember everything; I couldn't live without my notebook, and I have a little a-z book that I have all my passwords and addresses in too.

There are so many different styles out there you will definitely be able to find one that suits you. There are birthday books, gratitude journals, notebooks, goal and vision books. See which one makes you feel excited like you're five again, and that's the one for you.

Look for one that YOU like though, I have different books for different things because I just frickin' LOVE stationary, it makes me make squeaky noises.

When you introduce this into your life you will start to see the difference pretty much straight away and FEEL it too. You will feel so organised and have so much more head space. No more purses full of lists and bits of scrap paper. Dedicate space specifically for this.

Set Goals

Goals create structure. When we don't have specific goals in place then we can't organise our lives effectively. By creating something to look forward to and work towards it helps to give us purpose. When it's something that you really want you will feel the fire in your belly ignite, all the cells in your body will do a happy dance and you will have to stop yourself from making squeaky noises. You will just know this is the thing!

. . .

But what if you still don't know?

What I don't want	What I do want

The first thing we can do to get clearer is make what's called a T-Note.

Draw a line across the top of your page and the down the middle underneath the line, draw another line splitting it into two sections.

On the left column write ***What I don't want*** at the top and begin to make a list underneath of all the things that you do not want in your life. AND BE HONEST! This is just for you so you can't get it wrong.

Clear your mind, take some big slow breaths, and centre yourself, then write! Freestyle let it all out. When you know what you don't want, you can get super clear on the things you DO WANT!

Now on the other side of the table you have just drawn write the heading ***What I do want*** and write a solution to all of the things you don't want. This will help you to see what you DO want.

Look on the 'want to do list' and see which of the things gets you REEEEEEEALLLY excited? Which one gives you all the feels? Makes your gut and your spidey senses start shouting, "THAT ONE!" when you look at it?

Then that is the thing. And if you just know already then you just KNOW!

It could be a holiday to somewhere amazing, the Maldives, to see the Northern Lights, Glastonbury, New York. It could be your dream house. It could be to lose weight and be healthy. It could be to leave a relationship or change your job?

Whatever is it that is giving you all these feely feels, know that this is right for YOU! It does not matter if you tell someone something and they look at you with raised eyebrows like, "Really?". Remember this is your journey. I am SUPER picky about who I share things with now because as much as we love the people in our lives, sometimes when we tell them things that make us want to pee glitter, they don't find the same excitement in said thing as we do so they unintentionally piss all over our newly lit little bonfire, which dims the sparkle in our soul and makes us start to wonder if it is actually a good idea.

Keep hold of your sparkle at all costs my beautiful one. Choose the people who you know will GET IT to share your new dreams and visions with and if you don't have anyone you can always message me, and I will pee glitter everywhere with you.

When you Know!

Once you are super clear on what it is you want the next step is to visualise this thing and FEEL into what it would feel like for this to be happening or for you to have or achieve this said thing. The trick here is to believe and act like you already have it.

Imagine the feeling of driving down the road in your cherry red 8 series BMW. Feeling the warmth of the heated seat toasting your buns while the air conditioning cools your brow from the sun as it shines in through the windscreen and makes the glitter on your unicorn air freshener sparkle everywhere.

The biggest thing that the law of attraction responds to is *feeling.*

The best we can do is have fun and feel the absolute happiest and shiniest proper pee glitter feelings we can. This also means that if you're doing something that isn't making you feel happy then it isn't going to help you raise your vibration either. You are going to feel the exact opposite.

Here are some things that can help you:

Create an ideal story

Think of the thing that you want and write ALLLLLL about it. You can write about anything you like. Could be your ideal day, your perfect life, your dream business, anything that makes floats your boat. Or if you are more creative or just like having a doodle you can draw it. Or do both.

Create a Vision Board

Creating a vision board is more than just snipping out pictures from magazines, putting together a few pretty collages that make you smile and hoping for the best. It's a creative process, a powerful visualisation tool that helps you narrow down your desires and get really clear on how you want your dreams to look.

While you're setting clear intentions and goals, it is the Law of Attraction that magnetises and attracts you to the perfect opportunities and situations that you need to turn these dreams of yours into a reality giving you a powerful reminder of how *you* want to feel and what *you* want to do. It's all about you meeting the energetic vibration you want to feel for your life.

So basically, living your dream life before it has even happened. *Fake it till you make it*, as the saying goes, and it is so much fucking fun!

Our brain is an incredible machine, it is geared towards making us successful with every action we take. It trains our bodies to prepare for action! When we imagine ourselves preparing for an activity, our brains run through the process and send signals to the rest of our body to complete the action.

Use Visualisations

Although visualisation was regarded as a bit woo for many years, research has shown that there is a strong scientific basis for how and why visualisation works. It is now a well-known fact that we stimulate the same brain regions when we *visualise* an action, and when we physically *perform* that same action.

Try this with me. Imagine you're about to sprint somewhere (this would never happen in my life unless I was being chased by zombies, if you ask my daughter what happens when mummy runs, she will giggle and say, "She wees herself!")

Anyway...

Back to you getting ready to sprint. As you think about running really, really, really super-fast your brain needs to quickly prepare your body for when this happens. It fires up your muscles and pumps some adrenaline through your body to get you hyped so that when the pistol fires, you can shoot off the starting blocks as fast as you can but if you change your mind and decide not to run, this process has already happened. Your body believed that it WAS going to run.

This happens every time hold a thought, visualise it, feel into it and believe it.

According to the amazing Abraham Hicks, focusing on something for seventeen seconds activates a matching vibration. After the seventeen seconds the law of attraction brings you more thoughts that match. The longer you can hold these thoughts the more like to like energy you will attract.

SQUEEEEEEEEEE!!

Visualisation is nearly as powerful as performing the action itself.

Many celebrities and professional athletes use this visualisation tool all the time. Oprah Winfrey, Will Smith, Katie Perry, Venus Williams.

Vision boards are used to help you know what you want and to SEE what you want too. Seeing your goals daily will allow your mind to shift in the direction of your goal. Vision boards give you that motivation to take a leap of faith and push you to the start of your journey to smash your goals.

And even if you have setbacks, having that visual reminder will help you back on track quicker. They create a sense of happiness too; I often do a little happy excited bum wriggle when I look at my vision board.

I am on vision board number five now. I have achieved everything off my other ones. Things like opening my own yoga studio, running a retreat in a lighthouse, going to Glastonbury for winter solstice and earning over £10k in one month. Every time I looked at these visions, I would get a big belly flip of excitement which made me vibrate at a higher frequency and get a little bit closer to my dreams.

Vision boards aren't all about the physical, material things that you want in your life, they can be about feelings too. My last vision board had a lot of feeling words on there. Some of them were surrender, balance, making memories, light, and strength.

Practise Gratitude

Another positive and powerful thing to keep is a gratitude book. A gratitude book can have images and doodles about things you are already grateful for. A bit like a journal but just for the positive stuff.

Gratitude is a superpower emotion. When we have these visions and are grateful for them our subconscious mind assumes it is real right now.

Gratitude changed my life.

(Apologies in advance for this slightly graphic story I am about to tell, and some of you who know me will already know what I'm about say. So soz.)

A few years ago, when I was just starting out as a yoga teacher, I rented a room above a local coffee shop to run my classes, which I also shared with some other yoga teachers. Over the summer holidays things would get very quiet as the mums who came to my daytime classes had the kids off school so couldn't come. Which meant my income was hugely down.

So, I got a job in a local hotel as a cleaner. It was minimum wage at just over £8 an hour and it was honestly the hardest job I have ever done. I was (I thought) fit and strong at the time, but I found muscles I never knew I had and when I got home, I was wasted!

For the £8 an hour we had to strip the beds, make the beds, empty the bins, hoover the floor, polish the room, clean the mirrors, restock the teas and coffees, clean the bathroom, and restock the towels and toiletries. And we had to do two rooms within the hour. It was tough!

One day I was reflecting on this, I was grateful for having the job and the money. But I was MORE grateful for being able to earn almost ten times this amount per hour in my yoga classes. In the moment I felt consumed with gratitude. I can remember the feeling in my body, it was warm and felt like it made my aura expand outwards from my body.

At the time all this was happening I was cleaning out a very full bin in one of the rooms, I will never forget this moment for as long as I live. I was thinking about how this job in the hotel wasn't so bad, and how it had helped me with money over the summer etc. and literally as I had that thought, the binbag I was fighting with and had managed to finally dislodge from the bin split at the bottom. So I quickly put my hand under the bag to stop the rubbish going all over the floor.

All of a sudden, something cold and wet and weird slid out the bag and landed in the palm on my hand. It was wobbly and rubbery and then before I had realised what it was, (the only thing that it could actually be) I had LOOKED at my hand.

Sat in the palm of my hand, was a used condom, with no knot in the top, and the now cold slimy contents slowly oozing out into my hand.

I screamed. And then laughed. And then screamed again. And nobody came to help me, they were all working on different floors.

I did the funky chicken and borked my way to the sink while trying not to let the rest of the bag spill out onto the floor and bleached my hand.

I wanted to bleach my eyes. There are some things that you just can't unsee.

At this very moment I told the universe that ***I was ready*** for my own yoga studio, that I was grateful for all my clients and the money that I was making. And that I was grateful that I was working now but this was just a short-term window for me to fill. I began to feel into how I would feel when I had my own studio, to not have to share a room with people, and create my own timetable that worked around the times I wanted to do.

Two days later I got a phone call from my friend who has found a space I could use for my classes.

Four weeks later, I was in my very own first little studio.

High vibe list

Make a list of all the things you enjoy doing, like a go to high vibe list. Having a list of all the things you love to do helps to raise your vibration 3 times as much. Once when you are thinking about doing the thing, once when you are planning to do it and again when you are doing it.

It can also help you when you feel like you need to raise your vibration but feel so low sometimes you can't even remember anything that makes you happy. This list will instantly remind you.

Create a memories board

This is a fab thing to do with your little people too. All the things that you have ever done that made you smile, feel grateful or piss yourself laughing. This helps you to remind yourself how amazing your life already is.

Positive Affirmations

Add positive affirmations around your home, anywhere where you can see them. You can also set an alarm on your phone to send you them throughout the day. Or put post it notes with them on everywhere. Positive affirmations are very powerful little tools. They help to reduce negativity, fear, worry, and anxiety.

When these affirmations are repeated over and over again, they begin to take charge of your thoughts, kicking all the negative thoughts in the fanny and eventually changing your pattern of thinking and ultimately changing your life.

Like exercise, positive affirmations can actually increase the number of feel-good hormones in our brains. Positive thoughts create positive emotions, which can change our physiology and improve our mental, emotional, and physical health.

Make it your intention to think happy thoughts my beautiful one.

Be a Dolly Daydream

Visualise yourself already having what you want and the life you want. The more you can see yourself already having or doing the things you want the higher you will vibe.

This all sounds very good doesn't it, but what if you have no idea what you want?

What then?

This is very normal so please do not worry or panic if you have no idea what to visualise or what to put on your visions board

About 70% of my clients when they come to me initially don't know WHAT they want exactly. They just know that they don't want to feel the way they are feeling anymore.

Journal prompt

Here are some questions to help you get clear.

- If money was no object what would your days/life be like?
- What are your fears around the last question?
- What is your biggest dream, and how will you feel when you have achieved it?
- What is holding you back from your dreams?
- It is one year from now. What are the three changes you have made over the course of the year that you feel proud of?
- To achieve these dreams and desires list three habits you know you need to release.
- To achieve these dreams list three habits, you need to begin.
- List five qualities that describe how you want to BE over the coming year.
- List five things you want to DO over the coming year.
- Complete the sentence:

I believe that the reason I am here on this planet is to...

Ask, Believe, Receive

We have done the ask and believe bit, but when it comes to receiving the universe does not just hand over the goods. You still have a bit more work to do here.

Let me explain *Inspired Action.*

The Law of Attraction is based on a goal setting and goal achieving process that is reinforced by reprogramming your subconscious mind, but without taking action, not much will happen. This action, your inspired action is the key for you to manifest your desires and is equally if not more important than the other bits.

What is inspired action?

An inspired action is when you do something because you FEEL a strong inner urge to do it, like having a gut feeling. But it's not just a small action, it's a quantum leap towards your dream. This type of action is one of the most critical steps in the LOA.

It is all about doing something that brings you one big step closer to your goal, and doing it with that strong emotion, that knowing that this is the right thing to do right now. Once you have stepped forwards with the decision to take this step the energy behind it attracts the next step and directs you further in the right direction.

You may have heard that when you want to manifest something you should pay attention to the signs of the universe. These will show themselves to you as synchronicities, like seeing 11:11 or 22:22 on the clock, unusual coincidences, and the strong feelings that you have to do something that seems a bit unusual but FEELS so aligned and right that every little cell in your body is jumping up and down with excitement.

Often you can't explain where the feeling comes from or why you have got it, and sometimes you don't know what you should do with it, so you ignore it or don't bother taking any action at all. It's like a light bulb moment!

The Law of Attraction gurus say that the *Hows* are not our job, but we still need to have a bit of a plan. Not 100% of the detail or even the perfected end result, but we definitely need to have an idea about what we want to do next. Or nothing might happen.

Most of the time inspired action is something you do out of a positive feeling. You just want to do it, you have this inner urge and it feels totally amazing.

But, sometimes, it's not always like this because we have abundance blocks.

The universe will be sending us signs and synchronicities about which way we should go, or what we should do, but even when we see them, we still question them, especially if you are an over thinker or a worrier. Your inspired action is something that should happen intuitively, something where you should act quickly, not question it and just go with the feeling to do it. And DO IT.

Manifesting is a goal setting and goal achieving process that works on the Law of Attraction. It is based on the fact that you can programme your subconscious mind to accept and believe a new reality.

A reality created by you!

The subconscious cannot tell whether something is true or false and will accept this new reality as true and make every effort to bring you there. Your subconscious loves it when things are in balance, and everything is in the right place. You have to believe that your dream or vision will come true, then you start living as if these goals were already achieved. Act as if they are already in your life and then this will act as a signal to your subconscious mind that this is the place where you belong.

And then the magic happens. You activate the Law of Attraction.

Your subconscious mind (or the universe) will give you signs, attract ideas, bring people and possibilities into your life, you will have inspirational dreams, and epiphany or anything that could inspire the right action.

But you always have to act.

Without your action these signs are useless.

What's the difference between action and inspired action?

Inspired action happens out of a gut feeling, a deep inner urge that makes you do something positive that feels exciting. It is a step that brings you closer to your goal and often leads to the next important steps that will get you to where you want to go. It is something you FEEL inspired to do.

Society has made us feel like unless we are going a hundred miles an hour, and doing a million things a day that we are not good enough.

But often these are things like, working overtime, going to the gym, hobbies, running the house, meeting friends, helping out at a charity, scrolling through Facebook or Instagram, and NOT the things that we REALLY want to do.

We think too little before we act, an act not out of the excited inspiration we felt, we act because we think we should, we act because others do it, we act because we feel guilty.

These steps are NOT inspired action.

Inspired action can also make you feel a bit scared. Like a clench your teeth, squeaky bum kind of scared. This is because you are moving out of your comfort zone, and doing things that you have never ever done before, but you just KNOW they are right because you can feel it in your soul.

When you become aware of this and of the signs of the universe, and how to look out for people and synchronicities etc, then you are able to move towards and also consciously create your dreams and visions. And when you start to trust your gut and your feelings and trust that these actions are the *right* actions to take *right now*, and it *feels* right. Then *that* is the time to take inspired action.

Meditation can help you connect to your inner self on a deeper level if you feel a little bit clouded around making decisions. You can take an inspired physical action to manifest your desires by choosing to sit in meditation. The universe will see this and send you signs on what steps to take. This could be dream like visions, ideas or some of the things we have just mentioned, the synchronicities, the gut feeling etc. It is *so* important to use your intuition here and *feel* into things. Remember you cannot get this wrong.

Manifestation doesn't just work with your thoughts, there has to be a form of action on your part. This could be applying for jobs that suit what you're looking for and going to interviews. It could be doing the course to help you get the skills you need to do a new job or help you with your hobby or dream to revamp something, could be an interior design course.

Why aren't you taking action? Are you doubting the process? Do you either not believe you'll get what you ask for because you don't think you deserve it, or perhaps doubt the Law of Attraction? What steps do you need to take now? It could be going back to the mindset mastery section of this book and re looking at your limiting beliefs anything affecting your self-confidence and what things you truly do believe.

In 2016 I qualified as a Reiki master. I then had this sudden urge to help as many people as I could but didn't know where to start. And I knew that the people I wanted to help were mostly parent/carers who needed some TLC but couldn't work because of their commitments to their special needs children and they couldn't afford to spend any of their extra income on holistic therapies for themselves. So, I applied for funding through the Big Lottery group.

I had my vision, I got clear on who I wanted to help and why and completed my application to the Big Lottery Group. While I was completing it, I imagined all of the money that was going to help these women to take some well needed time out for themselves with no stress or worry about whether they could afford it or where the money was coming from to pay it. It was my gift to them because they bloody deserved it.

I imagined them floating out after Reiki treatments and going into the rest of their day with a calmer mind, being able to deal with so much more because they were rested and felt relaxed and de-stressed. Thinking of all of this made my heart swell and I was so grateful, I could feel my energy shifting and I wanted to make squeeeeee noises I was that excited.

I kissed my finger before I pressed the send button as I submitted the application. It was done. That was my inspired action. I now had to keep the energy high and feel into this energy every day while my application was being processed.

One night while I was in bed, I was visualising a brown envelope coming through the letter box addressed to me from the *Big Lottery Group*. As I opened the letter it said, "Dear Niki, Congratulations you have been awarded £9497 funding from the Big Lottery Group." and I swear I felt something shift. Not just in myself but in the whole fabric of the universe. It was like it happened. It was decided. That I had created that moment in the future and IT IS SO!

Nine days later a brown envelope was posted through the door from the *Big Lottery Group*. After I had finished pissing my knickers with excitement, I opened the envelope and the letter said, "Dear Niki, Congratulations you have been awarded £9497 funding from the Big Lottery Group."

I did it. Well, I believe I did it. There will be people who if I told this story to would just say, oh it's just coincidence that you got it, you were just lucky.

But I FELT it happen. And it was fucking AMAZING!

And this is why, I wanted to share this with you because if I can do these things and make the changes I wanted to make in my life, there is absolutely nothing stopping you from doing the same.

I am just like you. I have had shitty times and done things I am not proud of, but I am not my past. I have forgiven myself and other people for the bad things that have hurt me and affected my life because I don't want to have those feelings anymore. I want to feel happy and sparkly and in love with my life not looking backwards and making myself sad by thinking about all the wrongs that people have do to me, or the things I did I am ashamed of.

Why would I want to do that? It feels like shit to do that.

If the Law of Attraction is something that you want to bring into your life you need to choose the good stuff too. Choose the happy thoughts, and the loving memories, choose to get excited about your dreams and pee glitter everywhere every fucking day because nobody else can do it for you my sweet gorgeous soul.

Only you have the power to create the life you want and sometimes you will have to step forwards before you feel ready, but your positive mindset and messages from your body will be guiding you forwards with confidence and clarity in your mind and love and compassion in your heart to create your own inspired action.

PLEASE REMEMBER THAT THIS IS YOUR JOURNEY!

And what someone else is doing that works for them will probably not be the things that work for you. This is WHY you have to stay in your own lane, follow YOUR own inner compass and create the life of your dreams.

Live your best life and love the shit out of each and every single day because you just do not know what is around the corner.

Surrender to your intuition and allow whatever your experience is to be just that.

No more, no less.

Just yours.

The next pillar of my programme is all around embodying the magic of the moon, and it really does feel like that too. Magic.

27

PILLAR 4 THE ABUNDANCE OF THE MOON

This is one of my favourite things to talk about. Over the past few years, I have been paying more attention to the moon and the planets and how I have been feeling around certain times of the month, and so much suddenly made sense. Link this in with the Law of Attraction and BOOM! Magic!

I have always loved the moon, even as a child and all through my teens growing up I was such a *look at the moon* type person. It wasn't until I got a bit older that I realised that the reason that I was so drawn to her is because the moon is my planet. My star sign is Cancer and the moon is the planet that is linked to this star sign.

I really wish I had known years ago what I know now about the moon. For all the times when I felt like I was having an emotional breakdown over my over-ripe avocado or losing my shit over someone chewing too loudly, it was all down to the full moon. The sleepless nights I have running up to the new moon when my squirrels run riot in my head and the ideas and downloads just keep coming and coming ... making me feel like I have insomnia and am ready to change the world.

My intuition would feel so strong some days that all of a sudden, any confusion or self-doubt I had would disappear and I could see exactly what decisions I needed to make, and I now had the vagina big enough to make them too.

I want to show you how you can bring this into your life. Something so simple can really have a huge impact on your life. I also found that there was a feeling of connection with my beautiful soul sisters in my Facebook groups. Around the times of the full and the new moon we would all share how we were feeling, and it was so reassuring when we always felt the same, this made us feel like we were not actually losing our shit, and that we are all in this together.

For years I felt so alone and like I was weird (I know I am weird but weirder is what I mean). I felt a type of desperation, like there was a longing to understand something that was silenced inside of me. I felt frustrated like nobody else understood me and was super reactive to people around me who were also going a bit bonkers in their own way too.

I am going to be referring to the moon as 'she' or 'her' throughout this book as the moon is known for her feminine energy of the universe. She guides us inwards, to be closer to our emotions ignite our dreams and to discover our souls calling.

Let me start with a little bit of science and magic.

The moon has her own gravitational pull and affects the tides of the oceans and the seas, this is called tidal force. Us humans are made up of 70% water so when the moon affects the tides, she also has a strong effect on us too. This is why when there is a full moon and the rivers and oceans swell, you may feel more emotional, like things are literally be pulled out of you. As she affects the tides and makes them fuller and higher, she does this with our emotions too. You may have heard the word *lunacy*, and it comes from the word *lunar*. This is why they say some people go absolutely crazy on a full moon, because they can't control their emotions.

You may notice more sirens - ask any police officer and they will tell you that there are more arrests around a full moon. There are also more babies born on a full moon, and my friend who is a midwife said that when there is a full moon maternity wards will often have more midwives on shift for this very reason.

The moon also stabilises the Earth's axis, creating seasons. Research has shown that the gravitational pull of the moon slows down the Earth's rotation (how fast it spins). If the moon wasn't there the world would only have an eight-hour day instead of twenty-four! We already don't have enough hours in the day, can you imagine this!

She is not just a rock in the sky anymore is she!

The lunar cycle (The time it takes the moon to go from full moon to new moon back to full moon again) is thirty days, some of which she is visible, big and beautiful in the sky and others she hides away and goes dark. This is her showing us that we do not constantly always have to be standing in the light, and that sometimes we need to go inwards and nurture ourselves. She shows us that there has to be ebb and flow to have true balance in our lives and as women this aligns perfectly with our monthly cycles.

Before birth control and our busy, masculine dominated work places our bodies would sync naturally with the moon and we would have our monthly cycle either on the full moon or the new moon. During the time of our cycle our bodies naturally need to slow down as we let go and release. But most of the time we just push through because we make no time for ourselves, and society and our busy lives often do not hold space for us either during this much needed time of rest. So we battle through.

This is something that I used to do all the time. Putting everyone else before myself to the point of almost burnout. Nobody else seemed to notice so I just got on with it, because I didn't think that taking time out was productive.

Now I know that I have to slow down sometimes to speed up and when this sensation of forced energy appears and I am pushing myself into my masculine energy, into the do, do, do! I stop. I step away and I allow myself to be guided by my own energy. I move appointments with clients and clear my day and do the things that I know will help me to fill myself back up.

Self-love is not selfish.

Mother moon shows us that she does not always need to be shining at her brightest for people to realise that she is there. She has balance within her light and her dark side. This is truly the answer to everything in my opinion. Balance is key in all areas of our lives, if we could just give ourselves the love and compassion and kindness that we show to others, we would feel so much better.

If we allowed ourselves to slow down.

Take a breath.

Recharge and start again.

You wouldn't let your phone run out of battery would you? So why do you do it to YOURSELF?

In ancient times the moon was the marker of the passage of time, and our ancestors looked to her for insights and wisdom, using her phases for gathering, sharing and rituals. This shows that in the past we were so much more tuned into the moon. She who not only moves the tides, but also our energy levels and the water inner world of our emotions and dreams.

People have practised full moon and new moon rituals for centuries. But in modern day times we have so many ROUTINES in life but have lost the rituals along the way. Life is so fast paced for most of us. We have lost touch with the power of nature, with the natural rhythm of life, with an ebb and flow and at the same time our intuition, our insight, and our own inner feminine powers.

We have swapped ritual for routine.

Have a look at the meanings:

Routine: performed as part of a regular procedure rather than for a special reason

Ritual: something done with a purpose outside of the action itself.

The difference between a routine and a ritual is the *attitude* behind the action. While routines can be actions that just need to be done, like taking a shower or making your bed, rituals are seen as more meaningful practices and have a real sense of purpose. Routines are functional and are great for productivity.

If there is stuff you need to get done a routine is the steps you take to do it.

Rituals are also a series of steps, but these steps are carefully chosen by YOU and have a side benefit. It could be relaxation or to feel grounded or even just for pure enjoyment. Rituals help us to express our beliefs and our values, they don't have to be religious.

Think of how it would feel to change your morning routine into a morning ritual. Instead of doing something that you do every day because you HAVE to imagine taking this time to do something that you really WANT to do. Your perception would go from daily-grind to some gorgeous you-time.

Imagine waking up and pressing snooze instead of getting straight out of bed, so that you can drift into a slumbery relaxing meditation. Allowing your mind to wake up gently while becoming present enough to notice any thoughts or messages that you may receive while your brain is fresh and clear. The perfect time before the stresses of the day have crept in.

How would it feel to start your day like this?

You CAN choose to do this, instead of getting out of bed, brushing your teeth, making your bed, checking your emails, ironing your clothes. I'm not saying don't do these things because they may need to be done, but not straight away.

In the busyness of our lives, we have forgotten the importance of balance. That there is time to grow and time to rest, a time of high energy and a time to be still, gather and pause. We try to go one hundred miles an hour all the time, like life is supposed to be linear. But it's not.

We are also part of nature, and it is completely natural for us to have this ebb and flow. Some days we are full of beans, some days we want to lay face down on the floor. By working with the cycles and the magic of the moon, we can create deep self-awareness, we can create self-care, empowerment, and manifestation.

One of the moons biggest teachings is that there is a time to BE and a time to DO.

Even the moon doesn't shine at her brightest for 365 days a year, showing us that if we don't take a rest, we will have no energy, inspiration, or motivation when it is our time to shine. Everyone is always saying *how busy they are* or that they are *working flat out* and *never get a minute.*

Remember the saying what goes up must come down - when we don't have balance, we crash and burn out.

Burn out, stress, anxiety, and unhappiness are now at an all-time high, but it doesn't have to be this way.

Do you have a jam-packed social life or calendar for family things, or a mind that never switches off (like my squirrels), always taking care of others and giving your time and energy to others too? Tiredness, exhaustion, overwhelm, saying yes to stuff you don't want to, being taken advantage of – these are all signs that you are NOT in alignment and that you seriously need some self-care and time out.

This is where coming back into a cycle, a rhythm of taking care of YOUR needs, even if that's just twice a month, can make SOOOO much difference to your life.

Sometimes always being busy can be a subconscious distraction from what is *really* going on in your world. By always saying yes to things to keep busy because you feel like you *should* be doing something and feeling guilty if you don't, will quickly leave you feeling tired and overwhelmed. By giving yourself this time, it will help you to get to the bottom of what this is.

The new moon shows us this.

By disappearing from the sky for a few nights every month she shows us, without guilt, that in order to shine and be your best, to be full and present and powerful, you HAVE to take time out. Say *No*. Practise self-care, even if this comes in the form of a whole day of Netflix, naps and binge eating on the couch. If this is what you need, DO IT!

Withdraw into yourself to fulfil your own needs.

You deserve this time for you and as we take this time back, we begin to live back in alignment with the powers of the moon.

This was the start of my ritual journey.

Twice a month I follow new moon and full moon rituals which force me to look at specific areas and things in my life, to trust in myself by noticing what feels good and what doesn't and to help me realise what I really want.

It helps me to forward plan too. When I know there is a full moon looming and I start to grow fangs and horns and am dragged into the depths of despair by waves of emotion, I can go, "Oh it's just the moon." And it makes everything feel ok.

Moon Rituals are SO much fun. I have been doing them for about the last few years and I REALLY look forward to them now.

Ritual over Routine

Some routines can feel a bit boring like we just explored, especially when they are work related.

Rituals make something feel more meaningful, it makes things feel symbolic and gives life value and purpose. It is how we tend to our inner world and hear the whispers of our own souls. When we start living by rituals our lives take on a whole new meaning.

We start to live from the inside out.

It is what helps us to keep ourselves accountable and moving in the right direction.

The full moon and new moon are marker points in every month where no matter what else has been happening we can come back home to ourselves under the guidance of the moon to reflect, reconnect, realign and refocus.

The full moon is the midway point of the lunar month. It is when we get to see clearly what has stood in our way and where we can get clear on what we don't want in our lives anymore.

Tuning into emotions

As the full moon pulls the tide, she also pulls any emotions that we have been choosing not to look at or hidden in a box in a cupboard in your head, she pulls this out so that we let go of anything that we don't want or that shouldn't be in there anymore.

We often don't have a choice and stuff just bubbles to the surface because the moon is literally drawing it out of us.

When the moon is full our emotions are HIGH like the tides.

I bet you always tell everyone that you are okay when really you're not.

I used to do this ALL THE TIME!

But the moon won't let us pretend. She just pulls it ALLLLL out!

We often numb our emotions because they can feel too big and scary. We suppress them, deny then, even run and hide from them. We tell ourselves we are too busy and refuse to check in with how we feel and lose touch with ourselves and our own inner worlds.

Or we label our feelings and believe it's not okay to feel a certain way, like angry or sad or jealous, and think that we should always be happy and vibrant and perky. It's just not possible is it or normal?

I used to self-sabotage when one of these darker emotions would surface. Making myself feel like I was a bad person for having these thoughts and feelings, but the truth is, every emotion is valid and is there to show us something.

Take a look at this list of emotions below:

Jealousy – Shows you what you really want.

Anxiety – Time to wake up to your needs.

Shame – Letting others define who you should be.

Guilt – Letting others define what you should do.

Depression – Hidden anger.

Bitterness – Withholding forgiveness.

Sadness – What you love and care about.

Disappointment – You actually TRIED!

Resentment – Violated boundaries.

Insomnia – Two of your core beliefs are conflicted.

We are high and low. Good and bad. Light and dark. Happy and sad. We are not just one positive emotion all the time and the moon helped me to accept and realise that this is part of my nature too. It is so important that we allow ourselves to surrender to this darkness in order to step into the light.

Full Moon reflections

What are the main emotions you have been experiencing in the run up to this full moon?

What has stood in your way or felt difficult?

These are the things that are good to process under the full moon, dig deep, shine a light on the dark bits and let them go.

What has happened since the last full moon that has brought us any unexpected or unwanted emotions for you?

Full Moon Rituals

A really easy but still powerful ritual to start with is this one.

Get yourself somewhere comfy and somewhere where you won't be disturbed.

Light a candle and give yourself permission to have this time just for you. Put your phone away and turn off any distractions.

Begin to slow down you're breathing. Focusing on the coolness of the inhale, and the warmth of the exhale.

Now begin to visualise and bring into your mind's eye the things you no longer want or need in your life. These could be people, situations, jobs, relationships, anything at all that you do not want in your life.

On your next exhale release your breath slowly and visualise that you are letting go of all that needs to be released from your life.

When you have finished blow out the candle and imagine that you are truly releasing all you need to let go of.

As the full moon is the releasing time of the lunar cycle, a burning ceremony can also be extremely powerful.

For this ritual begin by writing down all the things that you want to release, each one on a separate line of the paper, or on separate pieces. This can be as many as you like, just keep going and get it all out.

Then when you are done hold the paper to your heart, and read aloud or state in your mind the things that you want to release before setting it alight and dropping it into a fireproof dish (safety first please folks!) feeling and intending the fire to burn away all that you want to let go of and watching the smoke as it travels upwards towards the moon, taking with it all of these intentions you have surrendered.

New Moon reflections

The new moon is all about setting intentions, it is a time for renewal, new beginnings and starting over. For planting the seeds of new ideas that you want to bring into fruition over the coming month. And these can be new ways of thinking and feeling too, creating new self-care routines or positive affirmations.

Here are some prompts for New Moon reflections:

Make a list of up to ten goals you hope to achieve in the coming month.

What thought patterns or past events do I need to detach myself from to create space in my life for this to happen?

Write down a list of intentions for the month ahead, what do you intend to do, have, feel or achieve.

How can you shift your routine to make your intentions more achievable?

What positive affirmation can you create that will help you stay focused and aligned with your intentions and goals. (If you struggle with this, go to my intentions section at the back of the book and use one that resonates with you.)

New Moon Ritual

I like to start my new moon ritual by taking a long soak in a hot bath, or a shower if baths aren't your things and allow all your worries to wash away.

Next, find yourself a quiet space where you won't be disturbed and light a candle. You can also bring any crystals that you have and create a mini little shrine around the candle. I also like to use oracle cards in my new moon ritual. I take the pack out shuffle them and put them to one side often with a piece of selenite on top of them to keep the energy cleansed.

Then I will meditate for about 10 minutes, or until my squirrels have had enough and are forcing my eyes open from the inside. Just simply breathing and noticing anything that is coming up.

I call in the powers on the moon and the Earth to bless and protect me and give me any guidance I need.

Then I write down my intentions. Sometimes I feel like I want to journal or write down any visualisations I have had too, so I allow myself to go with the flow here.

Then I fold the paper and place a citrine crystal (powerful for manifestation) on top on the paper for the whole cycle of the month. I look at it on the next new moon as see what has materialised.

Where is the moon at right now as you read this? What can you do to bring a bit of moon magic into your life?

And don't forget you can create your own moon rituals too. There are no rules to what you can and can't do. The things that I have included in mine are mostly traditional but sometimes I simply light a candle and process it all it my head while meditating and holding whichever crystals I am drawn to. Have fun with it. Don't overthink it and go with the flow. Your flow. Do whatever feels right for you and notice how you feel.

Feel your own energy shift as your soul remembers who you truly are, and every iddy biddy cell in your body sparkles and tingles inside of you. It's that feeling of knowing. Not needing to know why or how, just an inner confidence that you do not need to question as you align with your intentions and attract the energy of the universe towards you and your dreams.

You cannot get this wrong, it is all about your intentions and this is where the real magic begins. Right there, inside of you.

When I realised that I had the power within me to change my life, everything changed.

Using energy work, understanding my mindset, and embracing the magic of the universe I opened myself up to this new space that I had never even dreamy of.

A space where I felt like I belonged, that I was connected, that I could make my own choices and create my own life without needing permission from anyone else to feel or be or do ANYTHING!

I felt free.

I felt happy.

I had begun to awaken something within me that I had been searching for my whole life.

Connection to my Soul.

28

PILLAR 5 SOUL SPACE AND SPIRITUALITY

I have left this section until last because I believe that you have to follow a bit of a process to get here.

To softly peel back the layers of society and limiting beliefs that have kept your mind captured and closed for what is probably your whole life.

To understand that you can heal from the inside out.

To journey into the chakras and hear the messages your body has been trying to tell you to help you to re-align and heal.

To see with clarity the way your mind has been subconsciously programmed from being a child to how you now want to see the world through your own lens with your own views and boundaries.

To embrace the magic of the moon and the universe that has surrounded you without you even realising it, and to start to have fun going forwards to create the life of your dreams.

Now you have got this far you are probably a lot more open to the suggestion of connecting to your soul and recognising and hearing YOUR voice as the sound that you should be listening to, instead of looking outside for answers.

It's time to ignite your powerful feminine energy.

What is feminine energy?

Feminine energy is nurturing and intuitive, it is compassionate and receptive. When a woman is aligned with her feminine energy she is in complete flow with life. She does not need to be seen or in the spotlight as her energy is magnetic and draws people to her.

Her soft nurturing ways feels receptive and open, like you could tell her anything and she wouldn't judge you.

I want people to be drawn to me because of my energy and how I make them feel. I want to help other women ignite the fire in their bellies and express themselves in their most authentic and truest form, whatever that looks like for *them*.

To help them feel so connected and free and in tune with their feelings and emotions that they default to honouring themselves and others by creating clear boundaries and speaking from their heart and their soul. Without fear.

Making them realise that all they have ever had to be is themselves and this process I have created will take them on a beautiful journey to discover who they truly are.

It is when we allow ourselves to surrender and to just *be*, instead of doing all the time that we truly embody our feminine energy. When we slow down, become present and take notice of what we are doing and why, instead of pushing forwards to the next thing we feel like we *should* be doing, this is when we begin to hear the whispers of our soul.

(As I wrote that sentence the wind blew the trees so loudly outside my house, and it made a loud whispery shushy noise, like what I was writing was the truth. It gave me goosies!)

This hasn't come easy to me. After being in a narcissistic environment for most of my life it took a long time and a lot of inner work for me to be able to give myself permission to slow down without feeling guilty. I identified my worth by measuring the things that I was doing and how busy I was. If I wasn't busy, then I wasn't good enough in my eyes.

For a long time, I would play over old scenarios in my head of how I could have done things differently, or why things happened the way they did, but now I realise that what I was doing was putting my body and mind through the trauma of the experience again and again.

So much has changed for me, and hopefully will for you too after reading this book.

Here are a few of the different energy blocks that I have worked through on my healing journey that I want to share with you.

These might be things that at first make you feel uncomfortable when you think about them, so you brush them under the carpet or put them back in the box in your head for a while little while longer.

Letting go

Sometimes when we have been in a deeply emotional or intimate relationship with someone and, we have what is called an etheric chord attached from ourselves to this other person.

Although we are not physically with them, energetically they still have some power over us. When this person has hurt us, or we part ways with them we can still be energetically connected in this way.

Is there someone in your life that you feel this way about?

It could be there is more than one person?

I was introduced to a healing technique called Chord cutting when I did Quantum Holographic Echo Healing training and it blew my mind.

Using the power of visualisation, the client is guided into a meditative state and then talked through the process of releasing the attachment of this chord from their body, ultimately freeing them from the energy control of the other person.

If you feel there is someone in your life that you can't let go of, that you think about all the time and it brings us negative emotions or horrible flash backs of situations, then chord cutting may help you too.

Here is how it works:

Sit somewhere comfortably and give yourself permission to have this time just for you for the next few minutes.

Bring your awareness to your breath. The coolness of the inhale and the warmth of the exhale. Slow it down. In through the nose, then even slower out of the mouth.

Relax your brow, relax your jaw.

Now bring your awareness to this person. Imagine them standing a few metres away in front of you or if this feels too close you can imagine they are over the road or even elevate yourself, so you are floating above them and they are below you, unaware that you are even there. Whatever makes you feel safe and as comfortable as possible.

Notice instantly how they make you feel, and where are you feeling this in your body?

Which of the chakras is this chord attached to?

Now notice what this chord looks like. Is it smooth or bumpy, does it look like ribbon or rope, is it thick or thin? I really want you to notice all the details here. Take your time.

Now I want you to take a big slow beautiful deep breath in and as you exhale visualise all the emotions you have ever experienced from this person being given back them through this chord, because you no longer accept or want these. Now visualise the chord coming away from your body, like it being unplugged and shrinking smaller as it reels back and is completely absorbed by the other person.

As you see the chord disappear into their body they also begin to fade away. Slowly disappearing until they have completely dissolved taking away with them all the pain and hurt and emotional trauma that you have associated with them.

Place your hands over the space where the chord left your body and as you breathe deeply imagine a beautiful healing divine white light coming out of your hands and filling this space with while light and love. Do this until you feel complete.

Now bring your awareness to the soles of your feet, grounding down, taking bigger breaths and bringing your awareness back to your body.

Notice how you feel.

You can journal on anything that came up for you, or how what you saw made you feel if you feel like you want to dig a bit deeper here.

Forgiveness

I have already talked a little bit about forgiveness in the previous chapters, but it is something so important to me I wanted to recap and share a bit more about my experience.

It took me a long time to understand what it really means to forgive someone. I never understood how I could forgive someone who chose to hurt me. But throughout my journey and the amazing guidance from my teachers I realised that forgiveness is not about accepting or excusing the other persons behaviour, it's about letting go and preventing their behaviour from having any further hold over me and destroying my heart.

It is so important that you forgive others, not because they deserve it, but because YOU deserve peace.

"Forgiveness is the key that unlocks the door of resentment and the handcuffs of hatred. It is a power that breaks the chains of bitterness and the shackles of selfishness." Corrie Ten Boom.

Forgiveness sets you free.

It is important that you remember my beautiful one that you get to CHOOSE how YOU feel. Nobody else has this power. Only you! Choose to feel the emotions that raise your vibration and light you up. When anything surfaces that makes you feel the darker, honour them as they are equally valid, but if you can set yourself free with the key of forgiveness that YOU hold, CHOOSE this!

Forgiveness is not just for others. Sometimes we may need to forgive ourselves for things that have happened and this is where I discovered true self-love.

You cannot go back and change the past. Holding onto this pain is not healthy and will not make you happy. Forgive yourself for what happened, for the mistakes you made, for your poor choices, for not showing up the way you needed to, for not being the person you wanted to be.

You're human!

You did the best in that moment with the knowledge you had. Don't look back and think, "Oh my God I would never do that now." Because no you wouldn't. You are not the person you were then; you didn't know what you know now back then, and if you had you wouldn't have made the choices you made.

It is okay to make mistakes. Remember you can never fail because you always learn from the experience. Maybe not right at that exact moment but looking back you can see how much you have changed and how you are not such a different and better person.

Journal prompt

I would like you to get your journal and write down all the things that have come into your head while you have been reading about forgiveness.

Who has popped up, what memories have re-surfaced?

Write them down and then after each one write the words 'I forgive ...(Insert name)...' or 'I forgive myself' AND MEAN IT!

Really allow your body to feel it.

This may make you feel emotional but PLEASE remember that this is a good sign. When things come to the surface it is because they want to be seen so they can be healed.

Once the emotion has passed, it has been released.

It's time to give yourself permission to let go and create space for more positive sparkly energy in your body and your world.

You deserve this.

Intuition is the key to hearing the whispers of your soul

This my gorgeous soul is something that I could talk to you about all day.

Intuition makes me feel so magical and excited and connected to the universe that I honestly feel like I could turn into a little sparkly fluffy cloud and float off up into the sky.

Intuition is a deep inner knowing with absolutely no factual evidence to back it up.

It is the whispers of your soul. The butterflies in your belly. When your heart skips a beat. Gut feelings. Spontaneous wild and crazy ideas that make you FEEL like you need to do them NOW! It feels different for each and every person.

Intuition is a superpower

It is like knowing the answers without thinking but is uncomprehendible to the mind, and that's why people who have not experienced it themselves have a hard time believing it.

If it looks right but feels wrong, it's fear. If it looks wrong but feels right, it's intuition. And intuition does not lie.

Everyone has it

Everyone has their own unique sensing gift/power/knowledge, but because we are human and feel like we need to have evidence to believe things, we will often not trust any signs that come up because you can't back them up.

Have you ever had a thought or feeling that something is about to happen and then a few minutes later it does? It could be you were about to ring your mum and then she rings you. It could be you thought about someone being pregnant and the next day they tell you they are expecting.

The thing you need to notice here is how did this message come to you?

Did you FEEL it in your body?

Did you SEE a vision of it?

Did you HEAR it like a message in your own voice in your mind?

When you can recognise this, you can begin to pay more attention to it and start to strengthen your intuition.

When I first started doing this, I did question if I was losing my mind, so if this has already come up for you, know that this is perfectly normal to feel a bit batshit crazy here.

Know that you don't have to act on the things that are coming up for you straight away, but as you notice them tell yourself that your trust this to be right without the need to find any evidence, just allowing yourself to TRUST the message.

Know that your intuition is always on your side and always operates for the highest good. You can't have a naughty intuition that will make bad things happen to you and then go, "HAHA!" Until you start to trust it, and not have to have it proven to you, you won't be able to develop it. Get clear on how your intuition is trying to communicate with you and just go with it.

Have fun.

Nobody needs to know what you are doing, you don't need to say any of these things out loud to anyone if you don't feel ready.

Something that I noticed when I first started doing this was that I would get an intuitive message, notice it, it would happen and then I would doubt that I had the thought in the first place. Like thinking, *Did I just imagine that I thought that?*

So I started writing them down on the notes on my phone as they came up, and this helped me to prove to myself that it was really happening and I wasn't going mental.

Start to develop a relationship with your intuition. Trust it. Have fun with it. You will over time develop your OWN intuitive language and remember that intuition is just trusting your messages.

Using Tarot & oracle cards for daily guidance

Another way to use your intuition and ask for guidance that I LOVE is by using tarot or oracle cards.

More people than ever before are seeking answers and are being drawn to the magic of tarot.

The tarot cards are only magic because YOU are magic too.

The cards work as a mirror to your subconscious or shadow-self (the parts of yourself you would rather not look at so keep in the shadow).

The cards help you to see the possible and potential outcomes but with the knowing that you can still change your path at any time. You always have a choice. The answers are not set in stone, they are there as a wakeup call or a guide.

I used to be petrified of tarot cards. I felt like they had some devilish power that meant that if I got the death card I was going to die! The death card is one of my favourite cards now, it represents the end of a something and a new transformation taking place.

Tarot cards have been used for centuries, and there are different beliefs about where they came from. They are used mainly to give insight into the past present and future but are perfect for helping you make choices around pretty much anything that is going on in your life or for a bit of guidance if you're not sure which path to take and need a bit of a nudge.

Tarot cards have a very different energy to oracle cards.

Oracle cards are the friendliest type of cards to use. They give you clarity and guidance and even a new perspective. There are no numbers or suits or symbolism to remember like on the tarot. You simply pick a card and interpret the meaning as you would like.

Nice and easy.

The tarot deck is more direct and has a more intense energy. For example, the oracle card may say, "Connect to your intuition, it will guide and protect you."

The tarot card may say, "You are being deceived by those closest to you, you have known this all along, open your eyes woman!" Not in those exact words perhaps but you get what I mean here.

The thing to remember with any cards is that you always have free will. You always have the choice to interpret the cards whichever way you like and if you take any notice of them or not is *completely* up to you.

It's so important that you allow your intuition and higher self to step forwards when using cards, so that you make decisions from that deep inner place of knowing (but without knowing how you know).

Activating your own inner compass so that you feel it in your body, like you are being guided by your heart and your soul. Sometimes it can feel like your body is being physically pulled forwards, like it is wanting you to move towards the situation.

Your higher self is that part of you that is pure spirit and is connected to the whole universe. Your intuition is the voice of your higher self, and she always knows what is best for you. Your intuition will guide you and tell you what to do step by step and all you have to do is notice it, trust it and follow it. Which is the hard part because as I explained before, most of us don't trust ourselves enough to listen to the signs.

When you can tap into the loving guidance of your higher self you will become more aware of visions, synchronicities and feelings that make you feel and believe that you are on the right path.

Your higher self has faith that everything you do will turn out exactly as it should and that you are completely supported.

She believes in abundance and love for everyone.

All you have to do is get out of your own way and listen to her.

Now you know you are being guided by your higher self and your intuition before you start your tarot reading take a moment to sit somewhere quiet and allow yourself to be still. I like to hold the cards in my hands as I am doing this and intentionally connect to them. By this I mean simply say in my head, "We are now connected and in tune with each other's energy, I intend this reading to be for my highest good."

You can bring into your mind anything that you want answers to on guidance on here, you can also ask questions while shuffling the cards so that they become infused with your energy. If it is a new deck you have never used before you can look through each of the cards one by one, noticing how they make you feel intuitively, and if any messages come up for you. You may want to write these down.

When you are ready, shuffle the cards and cut the deck in whichever way feels right for you. Some of the cards may come out reversed or upside down. It is up to you here how you want to interpret these. Personally, I like to look at the reversed meaning, I see them as a different energy to the upright meaning of the card. When the card is upright the energy can be present and growing with the given situation.

When the card is reversed it can mean the energy is undeveloped here yet or that it is showing us things in a different light, either the opposite of the upright meaning or something that we can look to change to find a positive end result.

Remember you cannot get this wrong.

There are many different types of tarot spreads, and I have included a few of them here for you, some traditional and a few I have created myself.

You will find which one is right for you, or you may use different ones every day. It is totally up to you.

The main thing to remember here is to stay open minded, let your higher self/intuition guide you and have fun.

Most mornings I pick a card for guidance. I sit for a moment with the cards in my hand just intending for them to show me what I need to know, then I shuffle the cards and before I finish shuffling one of them will normally jump out of the pack. I like to look at the card and intuitively feel into the meaning. I look at the colours on the card, the pictures and expressions on the people's faces. Noticing if it triggers a memory or makes me think of someone or something in particular. Another thing I like to do after I have finished is to cleanse my cards. I do this my holding the cards over either incense or burning Palo Santo and intend for the smoke to cleanse away any negative energy.

You can also leave your cards our under the light of the moon and ask that she cleanses them with her beautiful energy.

You get to choose what works best for you.

I'm gonna say it again, YOU CAN'T GET IT WRONG!

Have fun creating your own rituals.

Meeting and working with your spirit guides

If you had said to me a few years ago that I would have been working with my spirit guides I would have asked you what special mushrooms you had taken. Now I tune into my guides energy on a daily basis and it feels really normal.

In fact, I friggin' LOVE IT!

Spirit guides are the guides, supporters, and advisors 'in spirit' who are right there with you on your journey through life but watch and guide you from the spiritual realms.

Other names for spirit guides are guardian angels, ascended masters, star beings, higher selves, ancestors, spirit animals, galactic family - there are so many.

Some people intuitively know who their guides are, and some people don't. I had NO idea who mine were, and to be honest I felt a bit bonkers at the thought of connecting with them. It was a whole other level of Woo for me, but I'm SOOOOOO happy I was found it.

There are many different types of spirit guides who all have different roles, purposes, strengths, and abilities depending on their purpose in guiding you. One of the main roles for any guide is to support you into coming back into harmony and resonance with the frequency of love.

When we come from that place of love, you cannot get it wrong. Whatever it is you are doing or being asked to make a decision on, if it comes from the heart, it is *true*.

According to the late Indian mystic Osho, love should be just like breathing, it should just be a quality in you. Whoever you are with or wherever you are, or even if you are on your lonesome, your love should continue to overflow, so that you yourself become love.

Just sit for a minute and give yourself permission to think some gushy thoughts of love. It doesn't even need to be about a person, it could be for a pet or the colours in the sky or for your life and all the amazing things you have in it (think clean knickers, your comfy bed and food in the cupboards).

Notice how this *feels*.

It should feel a bit yummy and maybe, just maybe, it has made the corners of your mouth turn up a teeny tiny little bit? This feeling is how your spirit guides want to help you to feel as much as possible during your human existence.

I first met my spirit guides when I was doing my practitioner training full Quantum Holographic Echo healing and it was one of the most magical moments of my life.

I was taken through a guided meditation by the teacher, I was a bit nervous, but she made me feel so safe and supported. She held space so beautifully and made me feel like no matter how bonkers my experience was that it was exactly as it was meant to be.

My first guide step forwards was Archangel Michael, he represented the masculine energy I was feeling into on my right hand side. I had heard of him but had no idea what he represented. He felt very big and tall and muscular. I couldn't see his face, only up to his shoulders, and I still haven't seen his face to this day.

He felt safe and protecting. Which after looking into his meaning is exactly what he represents. When I ask for guidance from him now he changes in size and how he feels to represent my own masculine energy or the energy of a client if I am asking him for guidance when doing a healing session.

My second guide was to my left on my feminine energy side. She appeared as the high priestess. She wore a royal blue velvet dress and felt very nurturing. Like I could lean in for a hug whenever I needed one and she would snuggle me in. She reminded me of my mum. That kindness and caring and unconditional love, but also with a, "I will tell you the truth even if it's not what you want to hear," type vibe to her.

She has long brown hair with a beautiful elegant golden crown perfectly placed on the top of her head. Her face is soft and gentle, with flawless porcelain skin and kind eyes. She changes in size and emotion when I ask her for guidance and will sometimes appear like she is sitting very far away from me if my feminine energy is not being honoured.

My third guide appeared behind me. She was very much taller than I was, and she placed her hands gently on my shoulders. A stunning Indian woman with long silky black hair stood there, she wore a light brown bikini style outfit with aqua blue and orange tassles on.

She felt strong and fierce and unfuckwithable, like a warrior princess, and I recognised her instantly.

She came to me in a Shamanic meditation I had done a few weeks before at a ceremony and in my meditative state presented me with the Munay Kai 13th Rite of the womb attunement.

She represented the giving energy. She showed me how much I gave to others by the size she showed up as. Sometimes she appears so big I can only see her ankles behind me. Like the green giant off the sweetcorn advert years ago.

My fourth guide appeared in front of me as just an energy frequency at first. I couldn't see anything, I could only feel it. It took me a few moments before I felt my gaze drawn downwards towards the ground and there sitting on the floor looking up at me was the most breath-taking white wolf with steely blue eyes.

I had seen this wolf many years before during a Reiki healing. His face slowly appeared to me and then he stared right at me. His eyes looking directly into mine, and nothing I did could make the vision change or move or disappear.

He represented my receiving energy. He showed me how I felt about what I was getting in return from people or situations. If there was no energy exchange he was very small and sometimes teeny tiny. Other times he would be normal size and sometimes super big and extra fluffy.

These four magical guides are always with me now.

I also have my mum, my dad, and my grandparents from both sides who I call in when I am doing a healing session as my angels.

I talk to my mum a lot. I have had numerous psychic readings and they have all said she is with me and wants me to talk to her more, because she misses our chats that we used to have every day or often multiple times a day. So now I waffle the ears off her.

I also call upon my ascended Reiki masters, shamanic healers, and my higher self when I am starting a healing session and ask for their protection and guidance. I can feel them step into my energy field.

I take all of my one-to-one clients through this amazing process, I also take them to meet their future self/Higher-self and receive messages and guidance. It is such a unique life changing experience and helps them to realise that they are so supported and connected. It gives them confidence and clarity in their lives and businesses and shows them exactly what they need to see that is right for them at that moment in time.

If you feel like this is something you would like to do there are details of how you can work with me at the back of the book.

MY FINAL NOTE TO YOU

I feel so blessed to be able to talk so freely about all of this now without fear of being judged or laughed at. I embrace it all and it makes me so fucking happy and feel so supported and loved.

It was one of my greatest gifts and I proper pee glitter with gratitude that I can now share all of these things with other women.

I have created my dream life using all of the things that helped me on my healing journey. I feel beyond lucky.

I am so grateful for all the amazing teachers, women, friends, healers, guides, soul-sisters, whatever they want to be called who have held space for me over these last few years on my healing journey.

These women have made me feel so safe and so loved. They made me realise that I could do anything I wanted and to trust in my abilities.

They helped me to make decisions from my heart and my soul and I chose to turn my pain in purpose, to forgive, to let go, grieve, surrender, to transform, inspire and empower other women to do the same.

To create the butterfly effect.

To create my own Feminine Energy Guide to share with you.

Thank you from the bottom of my big sparkly heart for being here and reading my words.

I hope you enjoyed our time together.

Sending you the biggest most mahoosivest squishy hugs filled with love.

Until we meet again.

Always be You!

Niki xxx

ACKNOWLEDGEMENTS

There is only one place to start here and that is with my unbelievably amazing hubby Mikey.

The man who has stood beside me and mostly behind me supporting me through this whole journey. My rock, my best friend, the person who I keep falling deeper and deeper in love with as time goes on. The person who has held me when I am crying thinking I am not good enough, the person who has always believed in me and pulled me out the cupboard on many occasions when I just wanted to hide from the world.

Thank you for always listening to me ramble at stupid o'clock at night when my brain is farting all over the place and my squirrels are giving me ADHD.

Thank you for listening to me and helping me simplify things with your wiseness and your hidden from the world inner guru knowledge that you have, that you don't even realise you have.

Thank you for putting up with me working so much sometimes and for calling me back when you can see I need to step away and take a break.

You are my hero. And I fuckin' adore you!

Thank you to Toni Ann Martin, Lisa McMurtry and Anne-Marie Mayers Clapp, for being such amazing and inspirational teachers. For holding me in such a safe and sacred space and for helping me to heal and grow.

Thank you to Heidi Fletcher for being there every day listening to my brain farts and super random voice notes, and for taking horrendous screenshots of my face when we are on a call which I'm sure she will use to bribe me with at some point. Lol!

Thank you to Lindsay Murphy, Heather Pollock and Rachel Daley for being my circle of sisters who helped me untangle my head and gave me different and honest perspectives on things.

Thank you to all the other amazing women in my life who have got excited and pee'd glitter with me along my journey ESPECIALLY my Woo Woo Tribe (you know who you are!)

And last but definitely not least my amazing children. All three of them so different for which I am so grateful.

Mikey Junior for being so frickin' clever and strong and showing me how important it is to stand your ground and follow your beliefs.

Nathan for being so true to himself, so bravely honest and having the wildest sense of humour.

Daisy for being the little arms that go around my neck, as our hearts connect I melt, bringing me back into the present moment. My little besty.

There are no more words left to describe my gratitude right now. Just the biggest most mahoosive **THANK YOU** from the bottom of my big sparkly heart.

ABOUT NIKI

Niki Kinsella is an unapologetically real, inspirational and rather sweary Spiritual Empowerment coach who is known as The Feminine Energy Guide.

Her down to earth manner and slightly bonkers sense of humour instantly makes everyone feel at home in her company, and she has supported and changed the lives of hundreds of women during a global pandemic by creating a safe and sacred online Facebook community for women to feel free, discover their true selves and follow their dreams.

Niki is a Reiki Master, Yoga Teacher, Meditation instructor, Shamanic Healer, Quantum Holographic Echo Healing teacher trainer and certified Life Coach. She now uses all of these healing modalities to help her clients and also to teach them to train in these techniques too.

Niki has drawn on the pain of being bullied as a child, a toxic narcissistic relationship, battling anxiety, depression and addiction and losing both her parents to create her purpose, and to help other women realise that they can change their lives too.

Niki helps women to discover the fire in their belly, heal anything that has been blocking them to feel excited about the future, and to believe in themselves enough to step forwards and lead a happy and fulfilled life, whatever that looks like to them.

Niki lives in Wallasey, England with her Husband Mikey, and three kids Mikey, Nathan and Daisy. She has a tufty dog called Bruce and a fish called Barry.

She loves anything spiritual, woo, and sparkly that makes her pee glitter, as feeling happy and grateful in life is what is most important to her.

How to find or work with Niki

Website
www.nikikinsella.com

Linktree
https://linktr.ee/NikiKinsella

Facebook
www.facebook.com/groups/thefeminineenergyguide

www.facebook.com/groups/thefeminineenergyguidethebookgroup